"...an impactful gui♦e an♦ personal story full of compelling stories an♦ useful tools for those of us who are lea♦ers an♦ continue to strive for bigger success."

—**Michael Strasner,**
Certified Transformational Coach,
Trainer, Best Selling Author of the book
Living on the Skinny Branches and *Mastering Lea♦ership: Shift the Drift an♦ Change the Worl♦.*

"... Crystal Church takes rea♦ers on a brilliantly woven journey into the a♦versity of life that when embrace♦ lea♦s to powerful breakthroughs an♦ realizations. Working with Crystal through this process as a powerful woman lea♦er, I learne♦ that I can be vulnerable an♦ express my willingness to acknowle♦ge nee♦ for personal growth. I have the ability to create a plan that is flui♦ an♦ thoughtful in or♦er to be successful upon implementation. THIS book is an exclusive look into the Dreamweaver process that I chose into, an opportunity to interact with the chapters an♦ steps to begin your own breakthroughs"

—**Amy McGuffin,**
High-powered CEO of Kittitas County
Chamber of Commerce, Wife and Mother.

"...Crystal Church has a heart of gol♦ ...but she ♦i♦n't always let it shine. She takes us on a unique an♦ engaging journey that is part personal story of triumph over a♦versity, part a step-by step gui♦e through her proven, proprietary 7-step process for changing the course of your life

an part fully transparent narrative of how she grew the self-love an*
*self-confi*ence to put her story out into the worl*. Every step of the way,
*Crystal shares can*i*ly with lots of love using her witty sense of humor
to genuinely recount the lessons she's learne an* is passing *own to her
*chil*ren an* to all of us."*

—Leah Lund,
Creator of One Whole Health Holistic Health Coach, Neuro
Nutrient Therapist, Certified Hypnotherapist & Rapid Transformational Therapist, "Reboot Your Brain & Train Your Mind
to be Your Most Vibrant Self."

The Evolution of
DREAMWEAVER

The Evolution of

DREAMWEAVER

7 Steps to Delivering on Your Dreams

CRYSTAL DAWN CHURCH

Chief Dreamweaver

ISBN: 978-0-578-72910-7

Table of Contents

Thank You,
Grandma Kathryn

For my Grandmother, Kathryn Gilmour, the single most important person in my life. My Grandma Kathryn was that person who, without saying a whole lot, supported me in every way. I always felt her presence and energy with me. She believed in me. She dedicated her life to supporting me. I do not think I would be here today without her. She has since passed and is looking down on me with great pride for how I have shifted my life.

I remember being with Grandma Kathryn in her garden, walking between the beautifully manicured rows, on carpet! (I am literally giggling right now.) Yes, on carpet. She loved to put carpet down on the dirt so she could walk barefoot and not get dirty.

There was also carpet in the carport, not for parking her car on, but for sitting and having your feet on soft carpet. She would let my cousins and me build blanket forts on the clothesline that would stay up for weeks. Many a daydream was birthed in there.

All the kids, and Grandma, too, would pick raspberries and strawberries right off the bushes and eat them without washing because she didn't use pesticides.

We would watch NBA basketball (Of course, she KNEW Michael Jordan was the greatest and loved the Seattle Super Sonics), Olympic ice skating, bowling, dog shows, *The Soupy Sales Show*, and *The Sonny & Cher Comedy Hour*. Now I am singing, "I Got You Babe." Our all-time favorite was *The Price is Right* with Bob Barker. She had a crush on Bob, and later in her life she would schedule her entire day around the 10:00 a.m. hour so as not to miss him. Grandma was sorely disappointed when Drew Carey took over. I was, too.

Grandma loved to scratch my back, lotion up my feet and let me crawl into the heated bed next to her, and I loved these simple times. I learned much later that I was mostly kicking her all night long in my sleep.

She had a wandering soul and loved to travel. I was her best travel buddy. Together, we saw the big Montana skies and enjoyed small road trips around Washington State every summer.

I knew we were headed to town for an adventure, seven long miles away, when she grabbed her purse, and stopped at the bathroom for a fresh coat of bright red lipstick. It is important to add that we ALWAYS timed our local adventures to happen over lunch, so she didn't have to cook!

All my prom dresses were custom made by her. She did not miss one sporting event or awards banquet. Her house was always a safe landing space for my friends and me. There were always smoked turkey legs in the fridge, fresh fruit and veggies from the garden, pickled pigs' feet, and buttermilk. She was gloriously, unapologetically Kathryn Gilmour.

I wrote this book when I realized I had a gift for dreaming, declaring, and delivering. When I was able to see how long I spent in the victim mindset, the whole world looked differently and I realized that those steps I had been taking during all the adversity through the years, were actually my magic formula for moving through the blocks that keep people from accomplishing their dreams.

When I think back to a time in my life when I could dream freely it makes me sad. I was little, around four years old. I can see my cute, pig-tailed, smiling face right now. I still live in the same small community in Washington State where I was born and raised. I can drive to the house where most of my early memories were created. Despite how the exterior has changed, I can vividly see, in my mind's eye, the little green house that I lived in with my mom and dad. What comes to mind for me when I think of that little house is how the outside seemed bright with the sun shining on it, and as soon as you came inside it turned very dark and felt chaotic.

During the time we lived there, I was able to dream freely, but just not in that house. I was afraid. My dreaming ability was based on the people I was around, my grandma, and locations. If I were with my mom and dad or in that little green house, I could not dream, but if I were with my grandma or in her home, I could.

For me, my environment had everything to do with my ability to dream as a child, therefore, I dedicate this book to my Grandma Kathryn, who provided a safe dreaming space for me.

Dedication

The Evolution of
DREAMWEAVER:
7 Steps to Delivering on Your Dreams

is dedicated to my Grandma Kathryn and for anyone
who is ready to create a powerful life, step into a victim-free
mindset, embrace self-worth, understand you have the power
to create your dreams, and live for yourself.

Acknowledgements

T hank you to my kids for being their unique selves and who are my most cherished creations. For me, being a parent is described by the textbook cliché phrase, "the hardest and most rewarding experience I have ever had."

They have taught me the most in my life and continue to do so EVERY SINGLE DAY. They are the best parts of me. Combine that with each of their unique traits and talents, and that makes them precious humans on earth. I love each of them with all my heart. When I think of them, a smile instantly comes to my face and my heart feels happy.

And, thank you to my parents. They absolutely did the best they could, with the tools they had during, what I am sure, was also one of the hardest jobs in their lives, parenting. They taught me what they knew from their perspective, just as I have done with my kids. They lived their lives with me in them, and I have done the same with my kids, and for that I am grateful.

Also, I want to thank all the people along the way, from my teachers to my coaches, to my lovers and my colleagues. I want to acknowledge mentors and friends who have given their hearts

The Evolution of Dreamweaver

to me. One immensely high-powered coach, Alicia Dunams, is why this book lives. She saw something in me that I did not know was ready to come out and that was this book, *The Evolution of Dreamweaver: 7 Steps to Delivering on Your Dreams.*

Foreword

"In order to love who you are, you cannot hate the
experiences that shaped you."

—Andrea Dykstra

All humans have a cross to bear. Meaning: We all live with
circumstances, traumas, trials, or burdens that we carry with
us through life. This phrase alludes to the cross carried by
Jesus to his crucifixion.

And, because humans are hardwired for negativity, negative
events have a greater impact on our brains than positive ones.
Psychologists refer to this as the negative bias, and these negative
circumstances can have a strong hold on our lives, our behavior,
and our decisions.

So how we view these negative circumstances will determine
how we view life.

xviii   The Evolution of Dreamweaver

And, as humans, we have a choice:

- Do we view this "cross" as a hindrance, or do we view it as hope?
- Do we complain about the cross, or do we see it as a companion to our journey?
- Are we a victim to the cross, or will we become victorious over our circumstances?

In *The Evolution of Dreamweaver*, author Crystal Church boldly writes of this evolution – from being a victim of your circumstances to honoring your story and ultimately becoming victorious.

Crystal uses her cross as a character in her story, an antagonist of sorts that she somehow makes peace with, forging a masterful story – not only her story, but the story of others, you and me, and how we can also triumph.

Is our cross something that happened *to us* or *for us?*

Crystal says, "for us."

Dreaming is the first step of Crystal's 7-Step formula for shifting our beliefs. It is the first step in creating. Have you ever dreamt of how the things that happened *to you* were really preparing you for your mission on this earth?

It is up to us as individuals to decide how we will view our circumstances. Perhaps they are just a relic or souvenir of our past, that we must climb over and overcome, on our journey to our ultimate life vision. Perhaps they are here to make us rigorous, resilient, and resolute. Ask yourself this question, w*hat goo* *has come from your circumstances?*

Crystal shares her cross as an integral part of her journey, as a gift, something that happened for her, and this becomes a gift to others. She bears her cross with vulnerability – creating an opening for you to be vulnerable, too.

And I ask you, as you read this book, and as you choose to decide how you will view your cross, how *were your circumstances a gift?*

If Crystal can see the gift, I trust you can, too!

Alicia Dunams,

Author, Founder of PeopleBetter™, Life and Leadership Development, and CEO of BestSellerinaWeekend.com and TheBookFunnel.com, Book Writing for Leaders

Introduction

This book is a combination of my story, someone else's story, and the 7 Steps that I, Chief Dreamweaver, Crystal Dawn, have found crucial in writing the new victimless story of my life. It is a story where I am victorious. Picture me as Rocky Balboa right now, arms raised above my head, pumping my fists triumphantly.

The wisdom you gain from reading this book will include:

- the value of dreaming
- the reward of making time for yourself
- the importance of imagination
- how to use creativity to heal yourself and your family
- how to move ahead in your career, start a new business, and increase your income
- how to break down any dream into a step-by-step process that is achievable
- how to reframe how you view yourself and others
- how to live judgment-free and in a space of radical acceptance

You will learn how to be a Dreamweaver with the *7 Steps to Delivering on Your Dreams!*

Doesn't that sound awesome?

The chapters that follow will outline, explore, and explain the process.

1. Dream
2. Declare
3. Design
4. Document
5. Detail
6. Delay
7. Deliver

Woven into the 7 Steps are the important words of those who have walked beside me in my transformational journey to becoming a Dreamweaver. Many people have provided support, love, and wisdom. One particular person, Lucas Mack, a friend and mentor, who I met while attending the life transforming Ascension Leadership Academy, has had a profound impact on my life and is the perfect person to include in the introduction to this book. Each time Lucas and I connect and talk, time passes effortlessly, and our conversations are deep, rich, vulnerable, and set my soul on fire. (Now playing in my head is Alicia Keys', "Girl on Fire." Head nodding to the internal song and using that energy to keep on writing.)

What follows is one of those connections between Lucas and me, captured via Zoom. Zoom is a relevant detail to share because this book was born during the pandemic of 2020, which undoubtedly will be etched into history for everyone in their own unique way. Because of the pandemic, a type of coronavirus, and its lethal spread, many governments worldwide ordered citizens to shelter in place and avoid face-to-face contact. Zoom quickly became a popular platform for communicating virtually "face-to-face." For me, the stay-at-home order provided a much-needed time to slow down, reflect, and gather my senses to tap into what was most important in my life. What emerged as being most important was being connected with those I love and cherish during a time of quarantine. Zoom worked well for doing that safely.

Below are the highlights of a conversation between Lucas and me that was very inspirational for me. I will include the important parts, starting with Lucas introducing himself.

Lucas: My name is Lucas Mack. I am a speaker. I'm a podcast host. I'm an entrepreneur. I've been a journalist. I'm a published author, and I'm a coach. I am standing for people to heal in this world and to help people say, "The pain stops with me, period." No comma, no other punctuation. The pain stops with me and it's time that we heal for all humanity. And that is what I'm working towards every single day. I am proud of you for going live (on Facebook) every day during this pandemic. It is amazing.

Crystal: Oh, thank you. I am having the greatest time sharing myself and having conversations with people. I know my wide smile is obvious while I am reflecting on the conversation that you and I had a long time ago that was the catalyst for me to create Dreamweaver Consulting. You encouraged me to be a Dreamweaver when I did not think I had anything valuable to share. A perfect example. I was so blocked I could not even create a website, let alone content for it. You did that for me. I fed you information of what I wanted to say and see on the website, and you kept saying, "That's perfect. It's fine. Just keep giving me content." You created the most beautiful website, depicting Dreamweaver perfectly. I was brought to tears the first time I saw it and still, to this day LOVE the website. You would assure me every step of the way in making Dreamweaver Consulting a real thing. "Go! Just do it. Launch. Go. It is perfect. You have all you need. You are powerful. You got this."

I was like, "... but what about ... no!"

THAT encouragement from you, Lucas, was so empowering. Dreamweaver is literally about taking those little steps, and the key is that you cannot do it alone. I mean, you can do some things alone, however, I needed you to be *my* Dreamweaver for this to live. I have been clear that I did not want to do this coaching/consulting like everyone else. "The Weave," my Facebook live program is an example of my desire to do it differently. The live show is not looking for the celebrity status person. I mean, "Of course, if Oprah or Brené called me and wanted to be on The Weave, duh!"

When people ask me to be on the live show, I say, sure, tell me your topic and send me a picture of yourself so I can create an event. The first questions from guests are always, "What's the content of the show? What is the focus?" My reply is always, the content is whatever you want to talk about, whatever you are passionate enough about that you want to share with others. During the live show, I am in Chief Dreamweaver mode, asking questions, enjoying conversations about leveling-up and addressing the "why can't *yous*." At the end of every 30-minute live show, I weave it all together with what lands as the profound message or realization from our conversation. It has been fun and a brilliant strategy to organically grow followers who relate to the conversations and the mission of Dreamweaver.

Lucas: Amazing. I am so proud of you. It is crazy. Here is what I believe is happening during this pandemic. You and I, and others like us are the people who were raised in the darkness and pain. We were raised in the fire, and then we healed ourselves. Our gift is that we can walk through this time of isolation with ease, where others struggle, because this is the most traumatic thing most normal people have gone through in their lives. And now people are requesting support. This is your time Crystal; you have the skills necessary to support people.

Crystal: Thank you. It feels incredible. Everything is being downloaded to me. I created the most incredible 7-Step process. I took the 12 Steps and traditions of Alcoholics Anonymous and put my Dreamweaver spin on it. I literally started by outlining what I liked and what I didn't like from my experience in my 12-step recovery process, and then wove into the framework, tools I utilized in maintaining my long-term sobriety.

The two people going through it as my beta testers are celebrating success. One person, who has been sober for about ten months, is getting loads out of it, going deeper into the stories and experiences that led to substance abuse. The other tester got sober the day we started and has embraced a new outlook on maintaining sobriety, which has historically been a struggle. I do not even know how to explain it, but it's freaking life changing. The first shift in the process is simple, choosing in without being tied to a specific sobriety date.

Lucas: Power is found at the Crystal Church.

Crystal: (smiling wide) Yeah. And people always say, "Is that a place, Crystal Church? Is that where you live?"

I am like, "No, that's my name. And yes, it is where I live, in me."

Lucas: Own your name. (This is foreshadowing one of the most important lessons for me, owning my story, owning who I am, owning my name.)

Crystal: Yes! For sure and own everything! For the first time in my life, I'm very aware that everything in my life has happened *for* me, allowed me to arrive at THIS place. People around me are really struggling with the quarantine of the pandemic, and I am feeling grateful for it. I am sad for those who are sick and losing loved ones, and I feel fortunate that has not been my experience. I am grateful I can provide support for those suffering.

The theme of all my coaching right now is – What are you going to take from experiencing a pandemic and keep it as new way of living?

Lucas, I was reflecting on another conversation between the two of us when I shared that I was transitioning out of the executive director position at Youth Services of Kittitas County, and you would lovingly push me to keep going. Just the other day, I was filling up my coaching calendar noticing the abundance of clients! I'm grateful for your consistent positive encouragement, and I am grateful for the intense experience of the Ascension Leadership Academy (ALA) we attended together. Which, by the way, the impacts of that experience continue to unfold and evolve in my life.

ALA was the catalyst for all my growth in the last few years. I am grateful to Jenna Phillips Ballard and her husband Brad Ballard for creating the leadership platform, and my friend Leah Lund (also a coach, whom I have reconnected with in her latest program, "Becoming Boundless") for inviting me to experience it. The bonds created with people involved in emotional intelligence and personal development work are strong and deep and continue to profoundly impact me. I reached out to Jenna while writing this book and asked her a couple of questions. You will easily see by reading her responses below why she played an essential role in my evolution.

Crystal: What is the importance of emotional intelligence in creating shifts in our lives?

Jenna: Emotional intelligence is the number one contributing factor to overall success. Being able to shift in an instant when the "unexpected" comes up creates infinite possibilities. Knowing how to lead your team in a way that keeps them inspired and enrolled in the overall vision is a superpower. The only constant in life is CHANGE, so being able to catch the curveball or knock it out of the park will have you be prepared for just about anything. We're all born knowing that we can be, do, and have anything. Lack of confidence, fear of the worst-case scenario, and scarcity are learned and taught. It takes discipline and commitment to be able to rewire this kind of conditioning and programming. Figuring out how to unlearn the belief systems that have been passed down from our parents is sometimes a lifelong journey. We either continue the cycle or we break it. And that is entirely up to us – regardless of who we marry, what's happening with the economy, the career we have, or which city we live in. Each interpretation we create is absolutely our choice. We have the power to write a new story in any given moment.

Crystal: What is your experience with being coached and coaching?

Jenna: Being consistently coached by mentors or leaders I respect has been one of the most important parts of my development as a leader. I'm a student of life for life. I will never stop learning. We're either green and growing or ripe and rotting, and that is true for as long as we're alive. If I'm not consistently growing, how can I possibly coach anyone else into that level of transformation? As a coach, it's incredibly important to walk my talk. If I'm not authentic in what I say to be important, it dilutes my messaging. Nobody wants a phony coach! There are a lot of people out there who say they can coach people into experiences they've never even had for themselves. Do your research and be discerning about who you decide to work with!

Crystal: What do you see possible for our world when people are supported and open to transformation?

Jenna: When people are open to transformation, it creates an environment of infinite possibilities. Being open for the sake of being open is the first step towards a new reality created by a shift in perspective. We can't create new possibilities with the same foundational beliefs that created our old paradigm. If we want a fundamental paradigm shift to take place, we must be willing to blow up what we think we know to learn anything new. If we're committed to being "right" then we make everyone else wrong. If we're open to looking at something from a different perspective, we open the door to a brand-new experience. This would cleanse the planet, heal lineage traumas, bind us together as a humanity, and end war as we know it.

My conversation with Jenna closes and her final comment is the perfect transition back to my conversation with Lucas where he shares his dream for humanity.

Crystal: What do you stand for Lucas? What do you think the most important thing is in accomplishing your dreams?

Lucas: The most important thing is courage. So many people I've talked to, especially analyzers, analytical minds, they say, "I don't know what my purpose is." I say, yes you do, you don't have a lack of vision or lack of a dream, you have a lack of courage. If you need people to walk with you for courage, then get people to walk with you, because no one's meant to do anything alone. The biggest thing to achieving your dream, becoming a Dreamweaver, is courage and courage defined is acknowledging fear and doing it anyway.

Crystal: Beautiful, I had two clear realizations after listening to what you just said. The first is the acronym for fear that fits perfectly here, false (F) evidence (E) appearing (A) real (R). The second thing: courage and being open to someone walking beside you. You and I collaborating on the creation of Dreamweaver is a good example of this. Out of your flip chart paper exercise grew Dreamweaver. Out of your shared process with me, the name Dreamweaver evolved. My mission statement for Dreamweaver grew out of our collaboration and I love it. It reads: Only with a victim-free mindset, and feeling worthy, are you able to create the life of your dreams. Magical. I was brought to tears in the simplicity and power of the process that birthed my tag line.

When I think about the *7 Steps to Delivering on Your Dreams*, I think about how it is supporting people through blocks of fear, unworthiness, and supporting them in shifting into a place of self-worth.

Lucas: That is beautiful. I have been thinking a lot about my healing journey for the past four years. When I was young, I had visions of what I was called to do in this world and through the pain and confusion and journey of life and all the things that happened, I got glimpses of those things, but they disappeared or vanished. During this pandemic, I have realigned to why I'm on this earth. It was like my soul forgot and I am remembering. I am realizing that what holds me back is getting distracted with things that sound good, but they are not mine. They are not for me. Those things are cool, and I honor and bless the people who do those things, but that's not me. My calling is me and my calling is for me. Your 7-Step process is so important to understanding our calling. It is how we reframe things and step out of the victim mentality.

Crystal: Let me move to the last question. I have a good play on words here. So, what is the golden nugget? See what I did there? (I am giggling because Lucas started a movement he titled, "The Golden Rule Revolution.")

Lucas: Here's the nugget: I feel like my purpose in this world is to bring the message of the importance of love. Through the lens of love, truth will come forth resulting in a personal freedom. When we do not feel judged, and when we surround ourselves with people who are safe, we start to take our walls down. When we feel love, we realize it is okay to unburden all the heavy trauma, pain, and confusion, and see through the cloudiness to release all these things that weigh us down. We speak our truth and when we speak our truth, that is when we experience freedom. We all want to be free. However, we keep surrounding ourselves in judgment with others, for others, and we get frustrated and depressed and feel a lack of hope because we do not experience what we genuinely want.

The formula is love, love that has no condition upon it. Love is a gift, a safe bubble, a safe ecosystem, a safe biodome for you to speak your truth and a safe place for everyone listening to your truth. Your truth does not need to be validated by anyone else. Whatever you believe to be true of what happened to you in the past, happened to you in the past. You do not have to calibrate it. You don't have to ask how did it happen? The fact is that it is still in you and not cleared out. To clear it out, you must speak it out and then you can breathe deeper. You can feel peace, you can feel self-love because you are courageous, and you can do things that you fear. This is where I believe self-love comes in. That is my message, where love is the precedent, truth will come forth resulting in our personal freedom.

Crystal: That's beautiful. And it's not necessarily something that I would say to a client in the beginning – I'm going to love you so much that you're going to feel comfortable. And that is exactly what I do. I love them unconditionally. I hold space for them to speak their truth. And oftentimes, for the first time ever in a place of no judgment, which is exactly what you talked about, this allows people to do the hard work of personal development and transformation. I am not tied to the results of their experience with Dreamweaver; I am tied to how I'll be in the relationship with them so they can feel that safe space and evolve.

Lucas: Yes. It is up to them to still take the courageous step and speak and do that work. But the fact is that you are creating that space for people to take off their mask and show the real person underneath. If every person, seven and a half billion people on planet earth, did that, we would live in the world that everyone wants to live in. And it's not hard, all you must do is stop judging yourself and other people to experience the fullness of love. Speak your truth and experience the freedom that you crave. There is no religion that you must join. There is no belief structure. You must jump in to free yourself, it starts by loving yourself and speaking your truth and then you get to experience freedom.

Crystal: I am so grateful Lucas, thank you.

Step 1
Dream

Have a dream. Find a dream.

Choose to be a Dreamweaver.

It is important that you choose to have a dream or be open to finding your dream. You must be a willing participant. The definition of dream I am using in this book is the one found in my quick Google search, the noun, "a cherished aspiration, ambition or ideal." The verb is "indulge in daydreams or fantasies about something greatly desired." The word "Dreamweaver" is used by combining the concept of dream with the (yep, you guessed it), the Googled definition of weaver. I chose the definition of weaver by Merriam-Webster, "one that weaves, especially as an occupation." Is that not perfect? Smiling my big, half crooked smile, I admit I am proud of this word *Dreamweaver* as a one-word descriptor for the *7 Steps to Delivering on Your Dreams.*

This is where we, as Dreamweavers, get to choose. If we do not have a dream, we get to have a dream, and by "get" I mean, it is our privilege and joy as a human to have dreams. Thus, we get to have a dream. I remember thinking this language is so weird. Trust me, it will begin to make sense as to why it is important to the *7 Steps to Delivering on Your Dreams*. In Step 1 of the Dreamweaver process we get to narrow our list down to one dream and choose to work on it. Yep, finding your dream is a dream. Wink-wink. There are no wrong answers.

I was born into dreamweaving. As mentioned in my personal thank you note, my Grandma Kathryn is who I proclaim as the original Dreamweaver. She was always creating something. She had a sewing room where she would produce beautiful clothing, quilts, wall hangings, and afghans.

Heck, she even went to beauty school in her 50s and received her cosmetology license. Add making people beautiful by styling their hair to her list of creative talents that she taught me.

Grandma always had a beautiful yard full of peonies, irises, and geraniums. Her garden was bountiful and famous for the carpeted rows between the produce. Yes, I mentioned this earlier, and it is worthy to note again, because she loved carpet everywhere! She loved to be in her bare feet. I guess she was grounding herself to Mother Earth before it was cool.

If she wanted to take a trip, which I always got to go on with her, she would dream up a way to craft something that was beautiful and had value. She would sell her gifts and save up until she could pay for the trip. This is a perfect example of being a Dreamweaver, taking something you are good at (or want to be good at), harnessing it and weaving it, so that you can have what you want.

As a kid I saw many places from the passenger seat of her car. I can still feel the joy in my heart as I sat next to her with the window down and the sunshine on my face. She loved a good road trip, and to this day, so do I.

Enter the story about Jake. First you should know, I will be sharing a parallel story of a kid named Jake to show the power of dreaming, declaring, and delivering. Jake always had a dream. Jake was a good kid. She was born into a family that was, from the outside looking in, seemingly very normal. Small town USA, mother and father, dogs, and cats. Eventually, and what is very typical today, a divorced family. Lots of extended relatives and immediate family around to support Jake in growing up in a single parent household. On the outside, Jake seemed incredibly happy. What was not seen was that Jake was being sexualized. She was witnessing inappropriate sexual activity, being spoken to in inappropriate ways, and being touched. Jake experienced incest as well as violence in the home, both verbal and physical. There was much disruption and despair.

Still, Jake was a good kid, thrived in school, loved the teachers, had lots of friends, and was popular. One of the remarkably interesting facts in Jake's story is she never really thought that this life was any different than anyone else's. Jake eventually learned this was not necessarily the case, not very quickly though. She was surrounded by families that lived in the same type of conditions, so chaos was the norm.

Jake, not being one to back away from challenges and conflict, was considered ornery and defiant by most. Here is the thing though, looking from the outside in at Jake's life, it is clear that this fighting spirit, the will to persevere, and personal grit is the foundation for getting it done in the face of adversity – in other words, becoming a Dreamweaver and delivering on your dreams.

And so, it is with the closing of Chapter One, that Step 1, choosing to dream is one of the most important concepts in moving forward. You must embrace your story no matter what it is, as part of your history, an important part of your life's journey and ultimately your purpose in this world.

As a young person, Jake knew nothing else but to embrace the story. In her mind all kids are going through the same experience of violence in the home – yelling, fear, and disrupted sleep. Jake's belief was reinforced by a close friend, who was also living a remarkably similar life. It felt like everybody in this small town was experiencing the same things, so it was very natural for Jake to fully embrace this life and its normalcy.

STEP 1 TOOL:
EMBRACE YOUR STORY

With each step required for evolving into a Dreamweaver, take the time to journal the answers in this book or purchase a journal to document your process. It is my powerful request that you answer the questions at the end of each chapter to get the most out of this experience and engage in the process fully. Each tool will be short, and all steps will build on each other. At the end of the 7 Step process, you will have discovered your unique zone of genius for living the life of your dreams.

(Picture that half crooked smile again, and me saying, trust the process. And then really, trust the process.)

When you were little, maybe five or so, what did you tell people you wanted to be when you grew up? Don't overthink this; write from your heart, what comes to mind right away?

1.

2.

3.

Now, with that same mindset, that same wide-eyed little person confidence, what do you dream of doing today? Don't overthink this one either; write from your heart. What comes to mind right away? You will notice that I ask you to do this often during the Dreamweaver process.

1.

2.

3.

STEP 2
DECLARE

Have hope. Have faith.

Be honest with yourself.

Shout your dream from the rooftops! Move your dream outside of your head and declare it out loud. Make a bold statement that you have hope and faith, and you are being honest with yourself about your ability to accomplish your dream. Own that you are a powerhouse.

Now, "declare" is a tricky word, and my experience with this as Chief Dreamweaver of Dreamweaver Consulting is that declaring a dream feels very scary. It is truly the most – well, besides having the dream, the second most important thing that you can do in the beginning of this 7 Step process to delivering on your dreams and becoming a Dreamweaver.

Simply declaring your intentions, out loud, on paper, to friends, and to a stranger makes it real. That is what brings the dream into the light and gives it a starting point. Whether you choose to declare it in private, on paper, or in your mind, there are many ways, steps, and levels of vulnerability. Seriously, that is what is frightening about declaring; it is vulnerable. I totally get it.

Declaring is part of the equation that adds up to equal the final delivery on your dreams. Many people create vision boards; Dreamweaver Consulting utilizes dream boards. Whatever you call the process, it is an effective way to incorporate creativity and visualization into manifesting.

After completing your dream board, it is recommended that you declare out loud what you put down on paper. This can be in person, a video with a friend, a stranger, or with a partner. Dreamweavers declare dreams after a group dream board session unleashing the power of boldly sharing the dream outside of your head. The dream becomes real and you have taken yourself to the next step in becoming a Dreamweaver.

During the Bestseller in a Weekend® course I attended with Alicia Dunams, I realized that I was taught to do many things that helped me create a path as a Dreamweaver. This realization came about during a partner exercise when I was asked, "What is a dream you remember most vividly?"

I replied that back in my childhood it was basic. I dreamed of living with my Grandma and getting to be in her space all the time. You know, to be next to her and crawl in bed and snuggle up to her every night. I remember this because I spent a lot of time with her. It was a time when I knew I was a good kid, well behaved, and happy. The dream was disrupted when I would have to go home. The good kid went away, and I was angry and confrontational, and my mom didn't seem to understand why. I loved my Grandma so much and felt so loved in her presence that all I wanted to do was be there with her. As a kid, that contrast of emotions was confusing.

Another question asked of me in the process of writing this book during the Bestseller in a Weekend® course was, "Is there a color you think of when you recall being in your Grandma's presence? If you were soaking in a color, what color would it be?"

My immediate answer was purple, which is funny because the Dreamweaver logo ended up being purple. The interviewer continued by asking, "Is there a smell that you would associate with your grandmother? Something that, when you smell it now, it reminds you of her?" Yes. I can smell it now. It's not a commercial smell that you could repeat, it is the essence of her humanness. What comes to my mind is lunch and the sewing room! I have NO IDEA what this even means.

In my 20s, I accomplished the dream of living with her, and it wasn't the same as when I longed to live with her as a child. I am sad that I did not have the same respect for her in my 20s as I did when I was younger.

Let's circle back to Jake's story and look at where she is in relation to the declaration of dreams. Remember, we talked about embracing your story. Jake had no idea that her story was any different than anybody else's so she embraced life as she knew it. It is the norm. Jake had many influential adults in addition to both parents that declared dreams and made them come true. If you could describe something, they could make it, or if they wanted something, they would get it. These guides and mentors also had tumultuous stories that they pushed through. This was the normal way of life for everyone in Jake's circle. They not only survived their stories but thrived in life. This positive role modeling was notably impactful on Jake's life.

Jake was taught resiliency, taught to dream, and witnessed people declare big things. Although Jake's mentors grew up in a different era, when being boisterous and declaring dreams was not as acceptable, they did it anyway. This was eye opening for Jake to see, even if it was personified in a quieter, more subtle way.

The chaos of Jake's life continued into the elementary school years and through the middle school years. There was a lot of drinking on one side of the family: quite different from the other side of the family. A mom and a stepfather on one side, and a father and many girlfriends on the other.

Eventually Jake had a stepmom. The domestic violence continued on Jake's father's side of the family, and Jake witnessed it. Jake was once again present for screaming, yelling, out of control behavior, alcoholic behavior, violence, mental abuse, and inappropriate sexual behavior. Jake was conflicted and confused by the contrasting sides of the family. Jake was fearful of her father, yet idolized him as well.

This interesting contradiction can be explained in Jake's story by noting that the eventual relationship between Jake's mom and her husband led her to feel left out. Jake felt her mom had chosen her husband over her. The confusing twist with Jake idolizing her father, despite witnessing abuse, was validated by the misconception that this was normal family behavior.

Jake's declarations at this early point in life were looked at by some as defiance. Although Jake had no understanding of Dreamweaver declarations, personal safety was created by aligning with her abusive father. Naturally, when Jake would go back to her mother and stepfather's home, her behavior was seen as unruly, irrational, and moody. This behavior was the result of being confused and traumatized by living in two such completely different households. Jake would be punished for bad behavior at her mother's house and sent to the bedroom to be alone. She subconsciously declared happiness would be a part of life, no matter what happiness looked like to others.

One scene in Jake's story is difficult to fathom. This time period is when life got very dark for her. Jake shares that at about 10 years old, the feeling of hopelessness, despair, and a lack of control in any area of life was so bad the only answer felt like death. I write with tears in my eyes because the thought of Jake thinking about suicide as a 10-year-old seems crazy and feels incredibly sad.

Because Jake spent so much time alone, being sent to the bedroom often, desperation took over one day and she found a knee-high stocking, tied it around her neck and put it over the doorknob of the door, all while watching in a hand mirror. Jake was very curious about the process of death and what it would look like to end the pain. She tried to let the neck muscles relax in an attempt to hang or choke out life. At the point when her face turned purple, she panicked and removed the stocking. This all took place in the bedroom while her mom and stepfather were in the living room, enjoying television.

Jake told no one of this incident and many others like this, and went on to appear normal, no matter how deep the despair was.

This was an interesting declaration for her, "If it gets really bad, I can commit suicide." That attempt became the first of many of Jake's attempts at ending life.

This chapter has been about declaring, having hope, faith, being honest and vulnerable. One thing to be noted about these 7 Steps is that they are listed in an order that is important, however, at any point along the way in declaring your dreams you may waiver, you may get lost and take detours.

STEP 2 TOOL:
BE VULNERABLE

Okay, here we go, grab your journal, or write directly in this book. Choose one of the three adult dreams you wrote in Step 1 Tool. Focus on this dream for the remainder of the book.

Spend some time free writing about your dream. Avoid editing yourself and your thoughts. Let them flow from that space inside of you, free of criticism.

Now, share the dream you are focusing on with someone. The riskier the way in which you share the better. The more accountability for your declaration you create, the higher likelihood you are to deliver on your dream.

Write down who you shared your dream with, and why?

Lastly, make a simple contract with yourself:

I declare that

I will _____ _____ (action),

by _____ (date).

And of course, shout this declaration, with the by-when date from the rooftops!

STEP 3
DESIGN

Responsibility. Making a move.

Doing something actionable.

Chapter Two ended with being vulnerable. Being vulnerable might happen much later in life for some, as we'll find out with Jake's story. The third step of 7, is design. You have dreamt it, you have declared it, now you get to design it. This is about taking responsibility, doing something actionable. In this step, you will break down your declaration into a plan. What does the plan look like? Writing it out, dreaming it out, thinking it out, speaking it out, any way in which you get it out of your body.

Some of the ways this step in the Dreamweaver process has worked for me include journaling about it, sketching a picture, drawing an outline, sharing with friends and family, sharing on social media, and even doodling about my dream.

I have my loving Grandma to thank for feeding my dream capabilities with creativity. That house was filled with creative spaces and project "stuff." There were drawers in the laundry room filled with ribbons, beads, tape (I loved tape!) wrapping paper, tissue paper, random objects for sparking a creative project idea. I even loved organizing those drawers, it was like a treasure hunt. Around the corner was a cupboard full of cards. Blank greeting cards for any occasion. My cousin and I would play post office with those cards all the time. Grandma always made sure everyone got a special card on each occasion, as well we all knew where to go if any of us needed a card for someone.

Even though the sewing room doubled as her in-home hair salon, it still held the magic. It had every kind of scissors you could dream of, drawers of lace, rickrack, silk ties, zippers, scraps of beautiful fabric, and more buttons than you can even imagine. The closet was organized with every type of fabric from silk to satin, to denim, and even terry cloth! That was popular when I was a kid. If you could dream up a project, Grandma's house contained all the materials to make it!

Often my dream process starts with a thought brewing in my mind. And when I am not in a beating-myself-up mode, feeling guilty, overwhelmed, fearful or in a space of victim mindset, my mind is in high creation mode, and I have many thoughts brewing.

I operate at an extremely high vibrational frequency and get, what some would say, are downloads of information and ideas about the incredible things humans can do. Declaring these downloads is an essential piece to the designing process, as is the timing of the declarations.

I have found that a project management program (I prefer Asana) is how I can store these downloads until it is time to declare them. I learned by burning myself out, that I can easily get too many Dreamweaver processes going at once and have a complete breakdown. The project management system is essential to staving off overwhelm and adrenal fatigue.

The design process for me happens first in my mind. As soon as I dream it, I declare it, and my mind begins to design it. Society's norms taught me if I work harder, faster and push myself beyond comfort, and grind away for years, I will achieve success. I have since learned that staying in the flow is strategic for me during the design phase. If I try to push the process of design faster than it is ready, it does not come to fruition, or at least not without pain of some sort. I have learned that when I push too hard, it sends me into a state of confusion that causes unnecessary stress and anxiety.

Now, let's transition to Jake's story and look at the design phase for her. Jake progressed into middle school, then high school, and continued to be an accomplished student while excelling in athletics. She was popular with peers and a bully to those who were not popular. She was learning the anger and violence being modeled in her father's home where it is normal to tease and joke and belittle people. Jake continued this bullying behavior without regard for others throughout high school and into college years. It is disguised with humor just as witnessed and taught at home; nonetheless hurtful to those who are the target. It is exactly what Jake experienced from her father. Jake is emulating the life she is living and designing her life through the lens of her authority figure.

Jake's father was notorious for creating situations during times that family and friends were together. Someone would always be targeted for his abuse, someone was always being picked on or bullied. The other people around turned a blind eye because they were fearful of being a target themselves. Nobody defended the person being bullied.

At age 17, Jake chose to live with her father. Remember she idolized him, and even more so when her father stopped drinking. Jake did not view her father as the reason she felt darkness inside. Unfortunately, the reality of it was, all the darkness inside Jake was about her father.

At that point, confusion was off the charts because how could the darkness inside of Jake be caused by her father? She could only see him as the savior. Her father helped her accomplish the dream of moving out of her mother and stepfather's home. Jake described the feeling of accomplishing this dream in relation to the body, "like when you have been holding your breath for a long time, and you finally exhale. Exhaling on an energetic level where you feel it radiating out of your fingertips. Exhaling while you're walking, and you can feel your hair loosen. Things do not feel so constricted and suppressive."

Jake did not even understand the concept of living life as she was constantly experiencing anxiety, acting hypervigilant and feeling chronically sad. She was living every day triggered, or in a state of fight-or-flight most of the time, all without being aware of it.

This is where Jake's story gets complex. Her father still had unhealthy and abusive behaviors. Jake had nowhere to go, felt unwelcome at her mother's, and was enamored with her abusive, but sober father. There was always constant inner conflict. Jake wondered if she should live with her mom where she would be safe, yet unhappy, angry and feel left out, or should she stay at her sober yet toxic father's?" Jake stayed at her father's.

It is important to note, that when Jake was at home with her mother and stepfather, the misunderstanding of behavior stemmed from their lack of knowledge around trauma. The science of trauma is a new scientific area today. Jake's parents were misreading trauma symptoms for bad behavior. There was no way for Jake to feel and process all the trauma. Her father was also unaware of how to process emotions. He had that old school, "Oh, come on, don't cry, buck up Jake" kind of attitude.

Jake felt safest by not feeling anything at all. She felt trapped – trapped in life, trapped in fear, and trapped in a mind full of mixed emotions and confusion. Her "go to" solution, the answer if it got to be too bad, continued to be suicide. This way of thinking allowed Jake to feel in control amid what was happening. At the end of the day, she still had control over whether to live or die.

Let us examine designing the dream and getting caught up in the stories around why the dream won't happen, and how taking responsibility for all of it is essential in becoming a Dreamweaver.

Jake's father modeled how to create power by reducing other people's power. Break others down to get a leg up. Jake was raised in an alcoholic environment and introduced to alcohol at an exceedingly early age. This is a crucial part of the story and why Jake struggled to see how to be a Dreamweaver.

At ten years old, Jake was allowed to consume enough vodka and orange juice that she could feel a warmth and fuzziness take over;

this goofy feeling would, later in life, be identified by Jake as being drunk. A life of getting caught up in addiction was inevitable for her. Amazingly enough, as those addictions grew, Jake was still able to dream, declare, and design dreams that did manifest, but it came with a price.

Being a very charismatic person, the life of the party, and a bully was a power trip for Jake. She used the manifesting ability to get free drinks at the bar, be invited to all the good parties, get great deals on drugs, and get breaks from law enforcement; all of which enabled her to sink deeper into addiction while crushing high school and getting a scholarship to attend a local college.

Jake became a parent early on in life, and, of course, addiction had an impact on her first child. She designed the perfect schedule to get through college while being a parent and one of the prices paid was the actual cost of her education. Jake took nine long years to graduate from college. Clearly a consequence of addiction.

STEP 3 TOOL:
ACCOUNTABLILITY & RESPONSIBILITY

Grab that journal dedicated to becoming a Dreamweaver, or continue to write in your book, and most important, trust the process. Respond to the following questions and prompts that make up the accountability and responsibility tool.

1. Write about a time in your life when your story (the story you wrote in your mind) negatively impacted your decisions.

2. Write about a time in your life when that same "true" story kept you from designing a plan of action.

3. What is one step you can take toward designing your current dream?

4. What has held you back from designing a plan for delivering on this dream?

5. What is one action you can take in the next 24-hours that will move you toward your dream?

6. Choose one step each day, that moves you closer to your dream. Do this for the next seven days.

7. Design a way to track your progress on your week one's steps.

STEP 4

DOCUMENTING

The next level of accountability.

Embracing creativity, precision, and study.

Step 4 is about documenting and accountability – writing it down, being responsible for it, going through it, not skipping over it, and creating a trail.

I am going to share how I am documenting this story right now, because it is important. I am speaking this story into Zoom and then I will have it transcribed, which is interesting because this is something I encourage clients in the Dreamweaver process to do.

Early on in my practice with clients, I recommended a client record himself while he was driving because the wisdom that this client had inside of him was profound. Every time we talked during the accountability check-ins, I was blown away by our conversations and the insight he shared. The client was stuck with completing his master's degree because he struggled to write the words. He tried the process I suggested and found much success.

I used a variation of this process with my Grandma near the end of her life. She had always disliked funerals and was very opposed to attending them or having one for herself. This changed for her about one year before her death. She decided that she did want a funeral, her way. She didn't want it to be with a "preacher man" as she called it, and she didn't want everyone crying. She wanted to pick the music, Amazing Grace, played by her favorite local accordion player, Karen, and she wanted to have her words read. So, I spent time sitting by her bed taking notes on all the things she wanted to say and filled in the parts of her life story that she was too tired and weak to write anymore. She had written pages and pages much earlier in her life that proved to be immensely helpful in creating the perfect Celebration of Life for her. Oh, and the BIG kicker of a request was that she wanted me, YES ME, to lead the service. Of course I said yes, and it was an incredible honor to host the most perfect final ceremony honoring all that Grandma was to so many.

I am totally laughing because of course speaking my story would work for me if I tried it. However, I often choose the harder route because, again, I had bought into the common way of thinking that unless you're hustling and grinding, you're not achieving.

I have learned that to the contrary, when I am in a flow state and letting things come to me naturally versus pushing, I am incredibly productive. It is in my flow state where I bend time, meaning I minimize the time it takes me to complete a project because it is being done in my natural rhythm, "my zone of genius," I like to say. My zone of genius is also where I weave similar tasks together to find time. Working from these two states allows for a more concise, laser-focused awareness, reducing the amount of time it takes to complete a task. I like to call this "making time my beotch!" Whatever your creative process looks like, embrace it. Forget the story you make up in your mind about how it "should" look and document it in the way that serves you best.

In college, I had this preconceived notion of how higher education was supposed to look. Because high school was easy for me, I wished for a magic wand to get my degree, because I wanted to skip the process of learning. I wanted to skip any required documentation from professors, yet I wanted to be impacting lives on a profound level with my degree. I wanted to show up only sometimes, take a test and get my degree and be as influential as Oprah and Brené. AND, most importantly during this period of my life, I also wanted to get wasted; be out of my mind, and party as much as possible. I loved the feeling of being out of control.

The magic wand theory created an interesting conflict. One part of me wanted to wave the magic wand to wake people up and activate them to be Dreamweavers as my Grandma did for me, but this would require studying and a deep dive into my interests. Counterproductive at the same time, I was putting as many substances into my body as I could to numb out. I avoided taking notes, passing tests, or documenting my interests about anything for that matter.

This is a good time to return to Jake's story and weave in the documenting step. Jake was a parent still deeply tangled in addiction. She had stumbled into a college major that included courses about alcohol and alcoholism and how addiction is passed down through the generations in families. Jake began learning epidemiology and genetics and how these health indicators impact communities and societies. As part of the curriculum of one of Jakes classes, she shared details of her life experiences for the first time among her peers. This opens the door to unlocking memories that will be important to documenting the story later in life.

Much time has passed since her college days and today we have a profound study called the Adverse Childhood Experiences Study (ACE). This study provides data that backs up the premise that what happens to us in childhood impacts us later in life. The health correlations are backed up by data to validate what many intuitively know about childhood abuse and other forms of trauma having a negative impact on our lives. Details about the study that can be easily found online will serve the reader well in understanding Jake.

The ACEs study *is* Jake's life, and college is where the darkness of her life became exposed. Jake saw sexual abuse, alcoholism, overeating, and all of those things that people do when they are functioning from a point of pain and trauma for just what they were, a coping mechanism from living a life filled with toxic trauma – a life with PTSD as a result of being subjected to and witnessing violence in addition to many forms of abuse.

A major turning point in Jake's story was a required college assignment consisting of a 60-minute recorded presentation on a health issue. She had already been opening pandora's box of knowledge by studying and experiencing many health workshops while attaining the college degree. This triggered memories and details of childhood abuse and flashbacks. Consequently, Jake chose a topic that was truly relevant during this time – incest. Jake took a deep dive into a very taboo subject.

The hour-long presentation was recorded, and each student was given a copy.

This stage in Jake's life is easily labeled as "the fight through it" stage. Fighting through life, fighting for life, and documenting the journey through the creation of this video, drawings, stories, and poetry. All these modes of documentation were instrumental in moving to the next step which was a big one. Jake delivered a copy of the video to each side of the family to disclose the familial abuse endured in childhood. She started by telling the story of a child who experienced this type of abuse and began to educate the audience on the topic. She was creative and used music, imagery, and guest speakers during the presentation to create a compelling and quality presentation and video. At the end of the presentation she disclosed that the child in the story is actually Jake.

Jake wanted classmates to understand the history of abuse without feeling sorry for her, and to understand what she had been going through the past several months in remembering the abuse, because it was visible. The flashbacks created chaos in Jake's mind, lack of sleep, and quick and massive weight loss.

Couple this with increased drug and alcohol use to numb the pain and fear, and Jake was a mess. By delivering these videos to the family, she was able to free the ugly secret, but not without a big price. Jake was shunned from the father's half of the family for "lying." The mother's side was in a state of shock because nobody had any clue what was going on. Jake felt alone again.

Of course, at that point, Jake had no idea how adversity is part of the Dreamweaver process. She started to become aware though, that there were some addiction issues going on. Jake attempted sobriety through treatment for the first time and it did not work long term.

She began to move deeper into addiction and justified behaviors because they were not preventing her from accomplishing dreams. Jake dreamt of college, declared going, detailed the plan to get a degree, documented it properly for professors and did graduate from college after several years.

Jake got married, moved, and had another child. She continued to have profound moments in her life, but without the watchful eye of family and community, the freedom of a new place to live invited more damaging drugs to enter Jake's life. She abused alcohol, marijuana, cocaine, methamphetamine, ecstasy, everything except for doing heroin, although she accidentally ingested heroin by unknowingly smoking it on top of marijuana at one point.

Jake adds in documenting this story, a strong belief in the power of the mind. She believes that being aware of taking heroin would have escalated into another addiction to that substance. However, because Jake didn't know the marijuana she was smoking was laced with heroin, her mind wasn't able to cling to it as something that was needed. Because Jake's mind didn't identify with doing heroin, she did not get addicted.

Jake's marriage was tumultuous, peppered with domestic violence, verbal, and mental abuse. At that point Jake was drinking and smoking marijuana excessively and chronically. She got a 'driving under the influence' charge, a domestic violence charge, jail time, and was mandated to go to chemical dependency treatment and anger management treatment – all while being married, employed, and parenting two children. This reinforced Jake's false belief that all was well.

This was a very hopeless time in Jake's life. She was haunted by the dialogue of committing suicide continuously running in the back of her mind. Jake's attempts at suicide would be categorized as sub-intentional – such as driving a car drunk, recklessly with no regard for consequences, and embracing the thought that doing so would be a way out.

Jake used lethal combinations of drugs and alcohol to get as far away from reality as possible, knowing that death was a real possibility, and not caring. Finally, she was given an opportunity to go back to her hometown, into the home of a beloved, supportive relative, only this time, Jake would do the supporting as this person was gravely ill. Jake's life was in chaos, deep in addiction with custody of one child and in the middle of getting a divorce.

This brings us to accountability – stepping out of victimhood to manifest your dreams. Jake was manifesting negative dreams and was unable to see that. She was calling the negative into her life by operating from a mindset of a sufferer, and this was holding her back. For Jake there was no problem because things were still being accomplished. She still had a job, still technically married, had custody of one child, while blaming the loss of the other child on her spouse. It was never Jake's fault. She had a huge martyr mindset. Then things began to crumble even more. Jake could not see that much more was available in life and that stepping out of the victim role was critical to achieving it. The way to the other side of chaos is right through the middle of it, armed with emotional intelligence work and the rest of the 7 Steps.

STEP 4 TOOL:
STEP OUT OF THE VICTIM ROLE

First, because I love the quick accessibility to google as a word lover, let me share the Google definition of "victim mindset" to give this tool structure. Google defined "victim mentality" as "an acquired personality trait in which a person tends to recognize or consider themselves as a victim of the negative actions of others, and to behave as if this were the case in the face of contrary evidence of such circumstances. Victim mentality depends on clear thought processes and attribution." Finally, Learner's definition of victim mentality, [singular]: "the belief that you are always a victim: the idea that bad things will always happen to you."

I would add that victim mindset is a block in progressing past the story of being victimized. I want to be clear that I am not suggesting that people have not been victimized; I am stating that the mindset blocks the steps to delivering on your dreams.

1. Go grab your journal, or simply write directly in your book. You are going to document important steps in moving forward.

2. What major blocks are coming to mind as you think about the rest of the steps required for delivering on your dream?
   List three:
   A.

   B.

   C.

3. Next, free write one paragraph for each of the three blocks you listed. Include all thoughts of why they are blocks, who is at fault, why it happened, how you felt and so on.
   A.

   B.

   C.

4. What story are you telling yourself about why you cannot achieve your dream?

5. Where in the stories you tell yourself are you seeing life as happening *to* you, versus *for* you?

6. Go back and reread the paragraphs you wrote and highlight where victim mindset shows up for you in the story.

7. Document any realizations you experienced implementing this tool.

STEP 5
DETAIL

Self-awareness. Self-love.

Self-worth.

This next step is about embracing the details of your story and seeing the gifts in it. You will begin to see that life is happening *for* you and not *to* you. My Grandma had a gentle way of showing me this lesson throughout my life. Oftentimes, it was not ever about what she said, it was how she was present and listened and found the gems of happiness no matter what. She led me to look at the bright side, which often meant skipping the details of the not so bright side. This quality is where my expertise is. It's how I speak with people after listening carefully to which words they choose to express feelings and ideas, and mirror back to them what those words mean. I lovingly interrupt stories that keep people stuck, the stories that stop them from moving to a place of finding the good things that are part of the story when we flip the script.

The details of self-awareness are critical to the Dreamweaver process. Embrace all sides of your story, seeing the positive and the negative as necessary experiences that you draw from to move forward.

My Grandma held space for me, which means she was a judgement-free and loving person for me, and that made it easy to be in her presence and sort through the details of my life. She spent time with me, listened and created an incredible bond by being fully present in my life.

I am intentionally recreating that safe space for Dreamweaver clients so they can deliver on their dreams in today's world. I am fully present and attentive during the coaching experience, listening without judgement. I am teaching clients that radical acceptance and judgement-free living that starts within ourselves. We must first love and accept ourselves without judgment.

As a young Dreamweaver, my aunt encouraged me to accept myself, not give up, and to look at the big picture. We would go for drives and talk, and she would comment about how wise I was. She called me an old soul and would tell me that I was people – smart and someday I would write a book. I remember thinking, *Sure, whatever!*

As I went deeper into emotional intelligence work, people were telling me that I have a great story. They would comment, "Have you ever thought about writing it down?" And I would think, *ya ya ya*. Now that I'm in a better place of self-worth, I can say, "Abso-freaking-lutely. I have a great story and I get to write a book!" It is a compelling story of how Dreamweaver became a thing, how it evolved. I have always used the 7 Steps, and I have always been a Dreamweaver. Now I have a label, a title, a process, and a book!

I feel like my aunt, my grandma, and many other influential women in my life, have all been instrumental in keeping me going. It wasn't until later in life that I was able to see any man as a role model instead of someone I could get something from, or someone I had to fight to protect myself from – the enemy.

Funny share from the Bestseller in a Weekend® experience with my writing buddy. During the interview process she would inter-ject and ask the most interesting questions. She asked, "If your aunt had a color, what would her color be?" I remember immedi-ately replying that Aunt Susan's color was baby blue.

Following suit, my writing buddy would then ask, "And what smell came straight to your nose when you thought of your Aunt Susan?" Again, I quickly blurted out, "Spaghetti." I got to spend a lot of time with her and her go-to meal was spaghetti. Her early Dreamweaver skills were creativity in economically feeding her family. She later told me that spaghetti was an inexpensive meal that she could feed everyone. Aunt Susan has a timid personality, thus the baby blue for her color.

Having very dominate male energy myself, it took me years to embrace the soft side of women. I went through a stage thinking anybody who was soft was weak. Today, I can see the value in that softness, and I am intentional in allowing myself to embrace it. I feel like I have softened over my lifetime, especially in the last couple of years, with emotional intel-ligence work as the catalyst. I am intentionally leaning into my feminine qualities of nurturance, sensitivity, sweetness, supportiveness, gentleness, warmth, and empathy. I am creating a balance with my go-to masculine qualities of strength, courage, independence, and leadership. This balance allows me to be an effective coach.

Returning to Jake's story it is important to note that Jake was medicating through life without self-awareness or the ability to notice details. She finally began to break through the many cycles that prevented forward movement. Jake moved back to her hometown, facing demons and the consequences of choices made in a life ruled by addiction. When she went to get a driver's license, Jake was flagged for not following up with court mandated treatment and domestic violence courses. Because she was still stuck in the victim mindset, everything was always someone else's fault – the court, the department of licensing, the police, the partner, you name it, anyone but Jake.

In abiding by the court mandated process, Jake returned to treatment. That began the phase of taking personal responsibility for all the details a life of addiction had created, including the fight to have rights reinstated. She began to look at divorce as a real and necessary step to support sobriety and mental health. To break the cycles of domestic violence, incarceration, drug and alcohol abuse, Jake had to face the demons. She embraced treatment, divorce, sobriety, and caretaking of an ill loved one, and thus began the work of embracing the details of the story.

Jake began to realize that childhood was not necessarily the same for everyone. She saw that the things that happened in her childhood had taught her resilience, which led to pushing forward and accomplishing dreams even in the most difficult of times. Jake noticed that people are drawn to, and gravitate toward her charismatic, complex, dynamic personality that is the byproduct of all her life experiences. She was becoming aware.

At this point, my book writing buddy, asked me if I would impact the world by delivering this book?

"Yes! It will be the tool for people to see what is possible when harnessing *7 Steps to Delivering on Their Dreams*. This book will be the catalyst to their self-awareness and the beginning of the journey to self-love and self-worth. I want my story to invite you into your own healing and then empower you with the tools and steps to facilitate healing. I will be fulfilled by dreaming, declaring, and delivering this book to the world."

My writing buddy from Bestseller in a Weekend® then asked, "And why the invitation, what are you implying? If there was one word or phrase to describe this as an invitation, what would it be?"

I, Chief Dreamweaver, Crystal Dawn, answered "an invitation for all people to see their worth and value."

As I continue to evolve and grow, to up-level my own self-worth and emotional intelligence, Dreamweaver will be the magnet that people are attracted to. I offer a leadership style that brings people on board, a leadership style that isn't based on a power hierarchy, instead it is a level playing field where we all have something to learn from each other. That is what I bring to the equation for value. I am leading people to believe in themselves, to declare what it is that they have not done, that they want to do before they leave this earth and then deliver on it.

I get to share the seven tangible steps to achieving the life you dream of all while I lovingly coach people through the proprietary process I have created. I get to walk beside people as they evolve into Dreamweavers.

STEP 5 TOOL:
EMBRACE YOUR STORY

In your journal, or below in your book, get ready to deep dive into the stories we buy into that ultimately hold us back. You are only a few steps away from the final step of delivering on your dreams.

1. Choose one block you wrote about in Chapter 4 and go into greater detail on the story you told yourself about the block. While writing, focus on your feelings around the story.

2. Once you have completed the story, spend some time embracing it in a new and fresh way and then doodle what comes to mind with your recent perspective.

3. How did I look, sound, and feel in the story?

4. What expectations did I hold regarding how the story should have gone?

5. What is different from the reality of the story and how I had planned it, or imagined it?

6. How does the present story look and sound like to me today?

7. What is the reality of the situation or the story? Can you identify gifts in the reality of the situation or story?

STEP 6
DELAY

Patience, The Power of the Pause

Okay, so as we roll into Step 6, you will see that in embracing your story self-awareness becomes particularly important. Step 6 is about delay, looking deep inside yourself, trusting the process, being in the flow, all while simultaneously moving forward to the delivery of your dream. Knowing that if it's meant to be, it will be, and it will happen on its own timeline. The dream will happen in the way that it is supposed to, which may be a challenge for you when self-awareness and accountability have not been high priorities.

As we become self-aware, we can see our lack of accountability and it is in this delay or pause that we can choose to reframe or rewrite the circumstances of our life to this point.

This makes me think about a little piece that my Grandma cut out of a magazine years ago. I must have been about 20 when she left it on my bed for me to read. We never spoke about the article, and

I kept it for a long time. I have since learned that the magazine cut out was a quote from the final paragraph in Joseph Epstein's book written in 1980 called *Ambition*. Here is the paragraph:

> *We ◆o not choose to be born. We ◆o not choose our parents. We ◆o not choose our historical epoch, or the country of our birth, or the imme◆iate circumstances of our upbringing. We ◆o not, most of us, choose to ◆ie; nor ◆o we choose the time or con◆itions of our ◆eath. But within this realm of choiceless-ness, we ◆o choose how we shall live: with purpose or a◆rift, with joy or with joylessness, with hope or with ◆espair, with humor or with sa◆ness, with a positive outlook or a negative outlook, with pri◆e or with shame, with inspiration or with ◆efeat, with honor or with ◆ishonor. We ◆eci◆e what makes us significant or insignificant. We ◆eci◆e to be creative or to be in◆ifferent. No matter how in◆ifferent the universe may be to our choices an◆ ◆ecisions, these choices an◆ ◆ecisions are ours to make. We ◆eci◆e. We choose. In the en◆, our own creativity is ◆eci◆e◆ by what we choose to ◆o an◆ what we refuse to ◆o. An◆ as we ◆eci◆e an◆ choose, so are our ◆estinies forme◆.*

This passage has meant different things to me at different stages of life. In my 20s, all I could hear was "We do not choose to be born" and "We do not choose our parents." Immediately my vic-tim mentality identified with this and began the dialogue of why me? Why did my parents not x, y, z. Oh poor Crystal.

Like I said, for some reason I kept going back and reading the piece for many years, and I remember in my early 30s rereading it and resonating with "We do not, most of us, choose to die," and I thought, well ... I have, several times. And why? Why do I keep choosing that thought?

Then, in my 40s I heard, "We do choose how we shall live," and profoundly I heard, "In the end, our own creativity is decided by what we choose to do and what we refuse to do." I love how this piece has been a major cornerstone in my evolution as Dreamweaver.

Looking at an update on Jake's story, we learn that after spending much time delaying many important life decisions because they were difficult, Jake finalized the divorce, embraced sobriety, and began to really look inside, reinvent, and step out of the toxic patterns. With this shift, jobs are now surfacing that are a better fit for Jake. She is working with people who are uplifting and positive mentors, people who believe in her abilities. Jake is feeling the forward momentum while no longer engaging in a life full of addictions. Success is becoming a part of Jake's arsenal of tools. She bought a house, got a new job, is earning raises, and creating positive life outcomes. These accomplishments are becoming the norm. Jake is beginning to impact people and the surrounding community on a profoundly positive level instead of the negative manner her decisions (impacts) previously had.

Jake is rewriting her story.

An important part of Step 6, delay, is having patience, pausing for results. It is in delay that the unfolding of your new story begins. It's in the emotional intelligence work of being grateful, expressing gratitude and seeing the gifts that you can wholeheartedly embrace your story. The storyline becomes more of a "what happened *for* me" instead of "what happened *to* me?" This is when the most commanding version of self comes out. This way of being is the key to delivering on your dreams.

STEP 6 TOOL:
REFLECTION

Grab your journal or write your responses below in the book regarding your feelings after you go read what you wrote in Step 5. Focus on how you felt in your story. Spend time in reflection first, only thinking about your feelings. Ponder and then write about these questions:

1. Do you honestly believe this story is true? Why or why not?

2. Is there one instance where you can see that the story might not be true?

3. How do you feel when you believe this story is true?

4. How do you feel when you believe the story is *not* true?

5. Where would you be without your belief in the story?

6. After time in thought, a delay, turn this belief or story around. Write it as if it is the direct opposite of what you believe is true.

7. Write out all your feelings about all steps leading to Step 6.

8. Do you notice any beliefs that limit you and your ability to achieve your dreams?

STEP 7
DELIVER

Give back.

Every dream I have ever delivered on, has my DNA all over it. It is a part of me, good, bad, or indifferent. So, Step 7 is the final step in *The Evolution of Dreamweaver*. This final step is about giving back to yourself and others for the greater good of the world. It is about delivering. It is about taking all the steps – dream, declare, design, document, detail, delay. Wrap all of that up with a big red bow on it and deliver it, right?!

You have experienced many situations in your life, many storylines you wrote during those situations, and if they were not positive, you have shifted during the process laid out in this book. You rewrote your narrative in these 7 Steps, and you have realized the keys to making your dreams a reality.

In realizing your dream, you began to share it. You began to focus outwardly, on others, because people are seeing you, people are watching you evolve, and it is empowering for you and for them. This creates a new sense of generosity and you are giving back on many levels. You are changing the vibration of yourself, other humans, and the world around you. You are creating the shift. You are the "change you wish to see in this world." YES! I love this quote by Mahatma Gandhi.

This is the gift of delivering on your dreams. People are drawn to that, and YOU. People want to understand how you did it and that process is exactly what this book grew from. How am I able to Dreamweave? How was Jake able to Dreamweave through all of that adversity? Jake used the 7 Steps and went on to ultimately be a nurturing and loving parent of three amazing children. She creates amazing friendships and relationships with people in the community and holds successful positions in the community, implementing programs that make a difference in people's lives. Jake reached a healthy point of emotional intelligence and mental health.

Jake continues to take chances, trust the process and level up. She continues to dream, declare, and deliver. Jake moved from feeling like a victim of life to seeing all the gifts that life has to offer. The delivery of dreams allows us to see that there are infinite possibilities, and when we are aligned with our highest good, we are open to receiving everything.

I want to end this part of the story by pointing out that this *7-step ream elivery process* is available to anyone, no matter what your obstacles may be. Jake's authentic, raw, bold, and vulnerable story is tangible evidence of no matter the adversity in our lives, when we embrace our story, rewrite it, step out of victim and into a powerful mindset, we get to embrace our wildest dreams.

This book is about me, Crystal Dawn, Chief Dreamweaver from Dreamweaver Consulting. It is about me giving you permission to crush your goals. It is about me sharing my version of the 7 Steps and 7 Tools so you can dream, declare, and deliver. It is about leadership. It is about people being able to recover from addictions. It is about people surviving and thriving after abuse. It is about people turning their lives around after being bullies and being bullied. It is about people struggling and shifting, struggling and reframing. It is about proof that these 7 Steps are a powerful process to dreaming, declaring and delivering the life of your dreams.

I want to thank you for following Jake's story through all 7 Steps.

Step 1 Being born into dysfunction and despair, embracing the story, and dreaming.

Step 2 Suffering abuse, being vulnerable, and declaring a dream.

Step 3 Being caught up in life, fighting through it, becoming aware of cycles, and designing the dream.

Step 4 Looking deep inside the self, shifting, sharing, and documenting the dream.

Step 5 Breaking cycles, facing demons, embracing the story, and detailing the dream.

Step 6 Pausing, listening, reinventing, having patience, gathering strength in delaying the dream.

Step 7 Evolving, sharing, giving back, and delivering on the dream.

I am ready to shine a light in all the corners of anyone's life who is up to the challenge, so that we can all positively impact our circles and the world. Dreamweavers believe that, with a victim-free mindset and feeling worthy, people can choose and create the life of their dreams.

If you haven't figured it out yet, I AM JAKE.

My father used to call me Jake when I was a kid. It was my nickname and now I claim the nickname Chief Dreamweaver. I do not hate anyone for the life I lived as shared in these pages as Jake. I fully embrace that this story is exactly why I have amazing talents as a highly intuitive transformational life coach. I believe that people are born into this world innocent babies and then life happens. I believe as the article shared by Grandma Kathryn goes, "No matter how indifferent the universe may be to our choices and decisions, these choices and decisions are ours to make. We decide. We choose. In the end, our own creativity is decided by what we choose to do and what we refuse to do. And as we decide and choose, so are our destinies formed."

VICTORIOUS

_1_

What a glorious moment it was when I finished the story portion of _The Evolution of Dreamweaver_. It was about 11:30 at night and followed two days of nonstop writing! I was alone in my apartment. I raised my hands in the air, cheered, screamed, yelled happy congratulations to myself and cried because it was the birth of something unique – me!

Fast forward to the two or three weeks after the evolution of my story on paper, I had been intentionally fighting (yes, contradictory statement for sure) my flow and trusting how this book would be received. Even though I have been pushing through feelings of nervousness, anxiousness, and fear, they were still keeping me stuck. Big clue Crystal – when you fight, you are not in the flow!

I realized, oh my goodness, of course I have many emotions right now, I just pulled off the ultimate declaration of taking back my power by owning my story out loud and in public. I was being off the charts vulnerable, so of course I was wondering what people would think. I do not get to skip those emotions; they are a necessary part of this process. One minute I wanted people to read the book, and the next minute I didn't want anybody to read it.

Yes, crazy confusion and a rush at the same time. I wanted to call everybody and tell them to read it, and at the same time, the thought of doing that scared the heck right out of me. It was profound how many emotions I had all at once.

It was during this emotional roller coaster of a time it occurred to me that I needed a safe group of people to read *The Evolution of Dreamweaver* first, before I released it to the world! Ultimately, I chose five women who I know and love, sent them the book, and asked them if they would be my peer readers of the really, rough draft. My peer readers are: Reality, Alice, Ori, Marlene, and my daughter Alex. I am grateful for these women, because at this time I still hadn't gone back and read the story myself after birthing it, let alone do any edits, I couldn't. I was physically and emotionally exhausted after writing it.

My specific instructions for my peer readers were to read the manuscript in its entirety for content and then go back and give me insight, input, likes, dislikes, anything that doesn't flow, anything that seems out of place or is questionable. The time between hitting send on those five emails and receiving their feedback was the most grueling wait ever.

Reality was the first to finish the book and she immediately connected with me. Being in another country, it was late at night for her. I remember her feedback because it was so impactful! I was worried that the story was not going to resonate with anybody. It was not going to make any sense, specifically, that the two stories (Crystal & Jake) would not make sense together.

Reality's reaction was completely opposite of the negative dialogue I was hearing in my head. This experience of waiting to receive feedback on my life story was a complete validation of the phrase, "trust the process," and validation of the important "Delay Step" in the 7 Tools!

Crazy perfect that in one of my most vulnerable moments of life, I was given the gift to experience the exact same concept that I had written about, and that I coach clients around. The power of the pause, the delay, and the power of trusting the process were all brought into play for me. The entire book writing process was another opportunity to use the steps that I shared, the profound tools that I teach. The book writing process is the ENTIRE process by which I have lived my life! The ultimate "cherry on the top" moment of trusting the pace of my peer readers led to another self-realization of how tricky the mind is and how I am susceptible to victimhood.

It is easy to notice when I coach other people and ask them to trust the process. I am often met with martyr mentality resistance. Now, I was falling into victim mentality with inner conversations of, "like whatever, you trust the process! Do you know what I've been through? Do you know how much trauma I have endured, and you want to take your time reading this book?!" Wow, crazy to reflect on the cunning ways victim mentality is triggered, and of course it was triggered. Playing the victim is my favorite personal development block to lean on!

As the initial feedback began rolling in, it was so revealing that I wanted to be able to capture everything the peer readers said and felt while reading *The Evolution of Dreamweaver*.

Yep, you may have guessed it, I decided another Zoom recording is how all these juicy tidbits of wisdom from my beloved friends would get woven into the final chapters of the book. The feed-back from these women offered in response to my story/Jake's story has been invaluable.

My intent in writing about myself separate from Jake, was for me to feel safe while talking about my story as another character. I also did not want to tell my story in a way that elicited judg-ment or sympathy. I was intentional with my words to not hurt or blame others or sound angry. I needed to speak my truth in a manner that I would be best heard, and the message would be best received. I needed to release the story of what happened *to* me, and embrace the story that happened for me, to create the leader that I am today.

Telling the two stories side by side, Jake and Crystal, was my way of doing that. I also feel that we all have tendencies to judge. I know I do, and the way the two story lines intersect at the end is a way for the reader to self-reflect.

My peer readers shared that they realized it was easy to judge Jake or blame others in Jake's story and feel proud of Crystal. It was an intense moment when the peer readers learned Jake and Crystal were the same person. I learned in self-reflection that inside of me will forever live both people, both stories, both struggles and both victories. The real aha moments continue to happen as my unconditional love for myself grows. Both parts of me feel the love. All the people involved in the stories feel love, because after all, it is only a story. It does not define me. It is not the final story and I get to rewrite my reaction to the story over and over and over, until I am free from any lack (lack of self-love, lack of self-worth) in my life.

Waiting for my peer readers to respond was the much-needed pause – Step 6 of my process.

After several days of the inner critic running the show, I was finally in a clear space in my mind where my ideas come to me by the millions. This is another reason why it is important for me to rest and recharge because my brain is always on, lit up and going full speed.

What you will read next are highlights of the conversations with my friends, and they were not scripted. It is important to let you know that my daughter, Alex, couldn't get on the Zoom at the same time as the other women because the timing didn't work for her. It eventually occurred to me, which evoked big emotions, that everything in my life has happened for a reason, and since I have two adult children that have gone through the Dreamweaver evolution right beside me, they get to have their own chapter. It felt perfect to know they both get to be part of this book's grand finale. I am going to give both permission to say whatever they want to say about this book because their story is also formidable. They will affirm other readers like themselves, that they are not alone in having a mother who has had a journey like mine. They prove that you can make good decisions based on how you choose to live. These two young adults have used good judgement to become incredible young people and take their lives in a completely different direction than I did. It has been fabulous to watch them both grow. They are both so much like me, so we did have some heated moments while they were growing up. They are both leaders. I'm a leader. I'm the queen of the castle. They wanted to be in charge of the castle. It's been a beautiful, beautiful journey. I have three kids total. They are all three absolutely loved by me. This interview is transcribed and included near the end of the book because one thing this book gets to do, is give women, men, kids, young adults, anyone really, permission to see that you have the power to stop undesirable generational cycles in families.

You have the power to make changes. Is it easy? No, I was 23 when my daughter was born, and this journey of self-exploration began. I am 52 at the writing of this book. The path of breaking cycles does not feel like this big, long, awful and drawn out thing, it has been a wonderful journey of lows that make the highs feel amazing.

ENLIGHTENMENT

The following is the enlightenment chapter of my story. You will learn where I am today and how I got here. You will soon hear from the four peer readers who, miraculously enough, ended up being, and I did not plan this, four women who didn't know each other before we jumped on the Zoom. What they had in common was being the first to work through the Dreamweaver process with me as their coach. The conversations that follow unfolded beautifully and organically.

I mentioned in the earlier chapters that attending the Ascension Leadership Academy (ALA) was a pivotal moment in my life when I was invited into a four-month intense leadership and emotional intelligence program. This program was the catalyst for many shifts and changes in my life. The first of which was shifting me out of a scarcity mindset.

ALA was expensive for me at the time. The training was in San Diego which meant four separate journeys there, and as a single parent, it was a financial stretch. Right away, there were many emotions inside of me triggered, starting with I cannot afford it.

Then my thoughts turned to – I do not have anybody to help me with my child, or my animals. I cannot afford to fly to San Diego four times for this supposedly earth-shattering leadership training that's going to rock my world. It took me a couple of months to say yes to this transformative experience. I understand firsthand how scary it is to take the huge step personally and financially to delve into your own development in hopes of a major life transformation. Trust me when I tell you, it was hands down why my life changed.

My life changed because I said yes to me. I made it work. Financially it was an investment in me that created debt. When I reframe that debt, I look at it as I would not be here as Chief Dreamweaver without investing in myself, specifically the expense of ALA. Not only did I do the training once, I did it twice in total because I went back to be a senior support staff member, a leader in someone else's journey. When you start, you're like, *Oh yeah, right, free labor.* No. That level of supporting transformation for others, and watching people evolve right before your very eyes, is the next level to facilitating your continued growth.

It is miraculous to be a part of creating a safe environment for other people to change their stories. Watching these profound transformations lit my soul on fire and it's why I knew life coaching was what I wanted to do.

To put the ALA experience into perspective for you, in one calendar year, I hopped on a plane, left my child, my pets, and my house eight times and flew to sunny San Diego (plus two extra times for fun) ten times! Holy Transformation Batman! I took one of my sons and I took my daughter (separately) to San Diego because that place became magical for me, I wanted to share it with everyone. I knew San Diego like the back of my hand. I could drive to the Seattle airport, park the car, get on a plane with one backpack, be gone for five to seven days, immerse myself in personal transformation, come back, reintegrate into the world, continue to be the director of a nonprofit and people could visibly see me shifting from the outside.

ALA is where I met Lucas Mack, and Marlene, who is one of my peer readers. Lucas and Marlene will forever be etched into my life as friends and soulmates who are instrumental in my journey toward enlightenment.

During this senior support staff level of transformation, I declared that I was going to make Dreamweaver Consulting real, bring it into existence. I was going to create a consultancy with a life coaching focus. I did not even know what it was going to be called. I took a leap of faith and trusted it would work out. On Martin Luther King's birthday holiday 2019, I launched Dreamweaver Consulting.

As mentioned before, I remember thinking this is not perfect. The website's not perfect; it is done, but everything's not perfect. Again, I clearly remember Lucas saying to me, "It's okay, you have enough; go for it." Thank you, Lucas, that has become a theme for me. I often share Lucas's wise words over and over with clients. "Everything doesn't have to be perfect for you to launch." That was a mighty step for me as a controlling personality because controlling everything would lead to perfectionism and stop my creative process.

Lucas' advice allowed me to be in the flow without even intentionally saying, "I am going to be in the flow." I stepped into the arena of *let's go for it* and see how it unfolds.

Reader, you can do this. You've got all it takes. It is important when you're taking big leaps of faith to be supported by people you can trust, who see you for who you are. That is why I am all about life coaching. I have a life coach to this day.

Dreamweaver started small because my plate was full being the director of a nonprofit that I revitalized with the implementation of an adult-to-youth mentor program. I started marketing Dreamweaver by literally writing the word, "Dreamweaver" on little pieces of paper, and wherever I would go in my community or on trips, I would take a picture of where I was while holding up the handwritten note, Dreamweaver. That simple sharing went on for six or seven months and little did I know I was becoming a trust agent on the internet by doing this. I highly recommend the book, *Trust Agents: Using the Web to Build Influence, Improve Reputation, and Earn Trust,* by Chris Brogan and Julien Smith. This book was where I first heard the word trust agent.

Then one day, someone said, "You really should get a business card or something, you know, like make it look a little more professional." And I agreed. I had really enjoyed the slow roll marketing because it was all I had time to do and it was fun to embrace one tiny step forward each day, but it was time to take another, different step.

It is important to mention that while I was in ALA, I dabbled in network marketing, selling toothpaste, face products and health supplements. Although, those adventures didn't end up being my passion, because there are no accidents, the experience let me know that my success with social media and network marketing, proved I was trusted on the internet. That is why I began to build my Dreamweaver presence on my personal Facebook page; people were listening and watching me on that page.

People were coming on board. They were interested in what I had to say, and even though my plate was full, I had the capacity to have a daily Dreamweaver presence.

That turned out to be one of the most genius accidental marketing techniques ever. Out of the positive momentum and feedback, grew programs based around the 7 Steps. I was transparent on Facebook during the creation process and that showed people who I was and what a life coach does. I made dream boards, which is the Dreamweaver way of doing vision boards, and shared them on social media. I did various small programs like, *journaling to reach your •reams, how to •oo•le an• move yourself forwar• in crushing goals on social me•ia, an• intention setting calls.*

Everything that worked for me in my life to create and spark positivity, I began to share with others in the form of a tool, all on social media. I began to realize that my way of doing things, how I accomplish things, my personal process is not usually something that other people do naturally. I had a gift in guiding people through the tools I was creating, and it was a high-powered experience for those participating. Looking back, I can see I have always been paving the way for this book, and these tools.

Last year, June of 2019, I was struggling mentally after working for seven years in the nonprofit world. When I became part of that organization it was an agency that was dwindling, basically dying, and I revitalized it with a program called Youth Services of Kittitas County Mentor Program. I was personally connected to this idea of a mentor program. I was born and raised in Kittitas County, and my mentors were instrumental in getting me through my life. I knew in my heart a mentor program was something that my community was ready for. The executive board of the nonprofit was not really impressed with the idea, however.

When I was invited to present the opportunity to them, I got comments like, "The former director, who was an outstanding human in the community tried this several times and it did not work. We do not see it working. We don't think it can be done."

Now, one thing you should know about me is when someone tells me it cannot be done, it fuels my fire. I am like, Oh really? Well I will show you. So, what I said was, "Can I try? Can I at least try to implement this mentor program?"

The board replied, "Sure, you can try. We don't think it'll work, and we certainly can't pay you because we don't have any money but go ahead give it a try."

I thanked them, said I would do it, and happily walked out onto the sidewalk and gave a big fist pump! Let the dreaming, declaring, and delivering begin!

Let me back up for second, I first heard about mentoring in a Rotary meeting. I had been invited into the Rotary by a mentor of mine. Rotary seemed like one of those groups I was not good enough to belong to. I had recently reentered the workforce after being three years in recovery from substance abuse addiction. I had no self-esteem, no confidence in myself, and did not feel like I belonged amongst the upstanding business members of Rotary. The minute my mind interpreted someone explaining the cost of Rotary as being difficult for me because my social economic status and single parent label, (Yep, you guessed it, that thing inside of me said, oh heck no you won't tell me I can't; I'm joining Rotary.) I joined Rotary.

Of course, this story ends up being one of the tools that I encourage people to employ. The tool is to step into the role or group that you want to be a part of and act as if you belong there, because you do belong there!

I joined Rotary by convincing my boss at the time that it would benefit our agency by creating important community connections, and boom, I was in! Money piece, check! My employer paid my membership and I got to attend meetings and interact with my community. There are no accidents, so Rotary members were on the original advisory committee for the mentor program and provided the seed money that launched it

I put myself around people who I felt were above me in some way, smarter than me, socioeconomically more stable than me, and I became one of them. I put myself in that situation and acted as if I belonged there. And guess what? I did belong there, and I pulled myself up to that level. I became a respected person in that group.

I even received a "Change Maker" award from Rotary. I kept asking myself what the heck is going on here. I began to build the mentor program and it is really where the digging in part of making a dream come true was beginning to form in my mind. That is also where I realized that when you tell me I cannot do something; it really makes me want to do it even more. And I do it.

Being born and raised in this community, one of the first things I wanted to do was transform the physical space of Youth

Services, into a place where kids and mentors would want to spend time. The building was old and run down and disheveled. It was uninviting; the rooms hadn't been painted in a long time. The carpet was old and there was plywood over a broken window in one of the offices. I reached out to basically everybody I'm related to in the community and said, "Hey, would you be willing to help me fix the ceiling, paint, replace a window and provide new carpet?" Before I knew it, people flocked to the idea of creating a space that youth could feel good about spending time in. I knew in that moment, there's no stopping a project whose time has come, something one of my mentors had said to me.

I was working my 40-hour-a-week job and gritting my way through this mentor passion project on the side. I couldn't get enough of the passion project! It started out as a two-hours-a-week commitment, then five-hours-a-week, and then 10, and finally 20 hours-a-week for a grand total of 60 working hours a week. Something had to give.

I kept going back to the nonprofit board reporting on my progress. They finally visited the space, two months later, after it had been completely remodeled to include brand new carpet and paint, at absolutely NO COST. The board acknowledged that it was an incredible transformation.

We never accomplish things that are hugely successful by ourselves. We always, always need someone to walk beside us, someone who shares our passion. At the agency where I was working full time, a student walked in the door one day, and said, "Hi, my name is Reality and I want to be an intern." And I was like, "Your name is what?"

And she said, "Reality. Yes, I know. I have heard all the jokes. My name is Reality and I am really excited about being an intern here." So, I invited her to sit down and talk.

There are no coincidences. Less than a week prior to that, I had read an evidence-based mentoring manual. I read it cover-to-cover very quickly, and as soon as I finished, I was on fire with the ideas from the manual.

Reality sat down and told me what her major was, Law and Justice with a minor in sociology, and said she really wanted to work with kids. I told her that I was working on a passion project and suggested she might want to work with me. For the next hour, I laid out my dream, and we laughed, and we cried, and we bonded in that moment over the mentor project.

Reality was instrumental for the next year and a half in getting Youth Services Mentor Program off the ground, all while she was finishing her University degree.

During the space upgrade I spoke of earlier, we literally ripped the carpet out by hand, loaded it in a trailer, hammered the nails down and prepped the floor for new carpet. We did the work physically and we did the work mentally. Reality created the logo and took direction on creating the processes. I found donors, mentors, and mentees. WE CRUSHED IT, TOGETHER.

It was amazing. Everything fell into place. In addition to my 60-hour work week, I am also a single parent. I was balancing two jobs and thinking it was so hard, and at the same time, it was lighting me up from the inside. One thing I did advocate for though, was money. Getting paid was important because this project was steamrolling just like I knew it would! The board could see this program was taking off and that I deserved compensation. I went back to the community because I knew I would be responsible for generating my own compensation, and I said, "Hey, here's the program I'm starting, and I need donations to get it going." Because I'm enthusiastic and I'm passionate, I am contagious in enrolling people into my dreams, and the money started rolling in. Sidenote: My kids tease me all the time about my volume and energy level. They ask, "Why are you yelling?" And I say, "I am not yelling, I'm passionate. I am excited. You've known me your whole life. I am not yelling."

That energy is infectious, and I have learned to use it to my advantage. And sometimes, maybe I am yelling. However, in that instance it was strategic and effective. People began to give me donations to do the work. They saw my vision. I was basically gathering donations to pay myself enough to keep creating this program in the hopes that I would eventually be able to work for the mentor program full time.

I dreamed that we would launch the program and impact the youth and the community on a profound level by putting an adult beside a youth in a committed relationship. A relationship where an adult walks beside the youth on their life journey. Mentors – not a savior, not a teacher, not a counselor – a friend who mentors by being a consistent and positive influence. It was working. I was fundraising, and the community was invested in making the program work.

This was around the time, in Washington State, when the I502 Initiative to legalize the use of recreational marijuana was on the ballots. This issue was something in my prevention job we were educating the public about. We advocated for voting "no" on I502 because of the negative impact it would have on our youth. The stance was that when we normalize marijuana, youth use will increase. Marijuana was shown to affect kids' brains negatively because the brain doesn't develop fully until around age 26. I will say that in my years of drug abuse, marijuana was easy for me to justify and held me back the longest. It kept me on the couch.

One of the things that the creators of Initiative 1502 wrote into it, was that a certain percentage of the tax dollars collected from marijuana sales had to go to youth substance abuse prevention and substance abuse programs. The very first state grant-funding source that Youth Services Mentor program received was from dedicated marijuana account dollars, which was so funny to me. I had spent so many years using marijuana, fought my way back, was sober, was working in the prevention field, creating a bridge to the Youth Services Mentor Program, and the money that would allow me to leap over full-time was coming from marijuana. Oh, the irony.

I remember the date of our first mentor/mentee match in the program, which is successful today. It was October of 2013. In retrospect I can see the Youth Services Mentor Program is where I first CONSCIOUSLY tested the theory of dream, declare, deliver. When I left the security of my full-time job for the mentor program and trusted that this was the right place for me to be, I delivered on a dream.

As I was settling in as the program coordinator of the mentor program, my former director of the substance abuse prevention agency, who was doing double duty as the Director of Youth Services as well, informed me that she can't be a director of both agencies, is going to resign from Youth Services, and recommended that I be the director. I said, "What? I do not know how to be a director."

She said, "Yes, you do. You keep doing what you are doing, and I'll be your mentor and you will do a fabulous job." So, before you know it, at the next board meeting, I became the director of Youth Services and that leap of faith turned out to be one of the most important leaps of faith thus far in my life.

This successful leap of faith gave me the confidence I needed to trust myself enough to know that I could be the director when opportunity came. Earlier in this chapter, I alluded to June of 2019 and how it was a quite possibly the most difficult time in my life. The backstory is that in 2013, I was implementing the program I created. I was the program coordinator. I was the outreach coordinator. I was the recruiter. I was the screener. I was the evaluator. I was the accountant. I was the fundraiser. I was ALL of that. And I thought I was fine with that because I was used to being addicted to something, and the work had become my latest addiction.

It was difficult to recognize the addiction to the project because it felt positive and not taboo. I was doing something good for the community. The program continued to grow. I learned to write grants. I learned to fundraise. In a noticeably short time, budgets went from $20,000 to $50,000 to $90,000 to $150,000, and the highest budget ended up at $300,000 right before my mental health breakdown.

Remember 2013 was the very first match of mentor to mentee, so that was a fast and furious growth process in seven short years.

I only had one 10 hour-a-week staff member until 2015 when I gathered enough funding for one full time staff member, and finally in 2019, three staff members.

In June of 2019, I hit the wall for the final time. I had felt very burnt out and overwhelmed for years; it seemed normal. I did not understand that I was pushing myself too hard. I wanted this to happen, and I knew that if I worked hard enough that I could reach my goal, I could make it work. I had determination and I did make it work, and I do not regret it because I learned so much along the way. I learned how to soften my edges. I learned how to be in my feminine versus my masculine. I had many versions of a board of directors because of my leadership styles that evolved over time, and how I led didn't work for everyone. Youth Services continues to be one of my greatest learning experiences ever. When I met Alice, who is the current director, and part of my peer reading group, I knew that she was the one capable of taking over the program.

Unfortunately, Alice worked somewhere else at the time and we had no funding to bring her on. Less than six months later, I received another grant and was able to hire her from her current agency. I brought her on board as the person under me and valued her like she'd never been valued before, which is an effective way to empower people. Youth Services paid her like she'd never been paid before, as well.

It was another one of those instant connections and we began to take everything that was in my head about Youth Services and put it into processes. Alice was a genius at process! A natural consequence was that she was learning how to be the director. I didn't intentionally plan that in the beginning. It is, however, how it naturally played out. Alice is a process expert because of her time as a Marine and was the right person to partner with me in the next evolution of my life and of Youth Services.

Without her knowledge of adverse childhood experiences, her own personal experience with trauma, I would not have made it through the mental health crisis that happened in June of 2019.

I was distraught and hopeless, and those old feelings of that familiar relationship with suicide came back. It wasn't a feeling accompanied by a plan; however, it was an intense and debilitating feeling. It was that feeling that was all too familiar and I didn't want it back. I didn't want that ongoing relationship. I didn't want to feel that desperate. With much encouragement from Alice and others in my support circle, I went to the board and said that I needed 30 days paid leave to get my head together. I literally felt like I could not think. My brain was so overworked that my adrenals were blown out. It was a horrible feeling, almost like I had a concussion.

Two months after Alice came on board, my legs literally gave out. I twisted my ankle and fell while I was simply standing at my computer. I had no idea why this happened at the time, and it was not until I began to write this chapter that I realized my body was giving out.

In April and May of 2019, I would cry at the drop of a hat. I was a mess. Thankfully, the board approved my paid leave, because contrary to my belief, they saw value in me. Alice stepped in as director for those 30 days, which was beyond helpful for me, and difficult for Alice. The gift was it was a sneak peek into what she was capable of, and what her life would look like in 2020.

As a workaholic, taking time off was hard. Several times in the first week Alice would threaten, "I'm going to change your password if I see you in the email working again." She would lovingly and gently coach me the same way I had coached her in the past, and tell me that the only way I was going to recover from this mental health crisis (which she constantly assured me was nothing to be ashamed of) was to disconnect from the organization completely. No email. No phone calls. Alice directed me that the only phone call I was allowed would be to her, and it was not to be about work, it was about support only. No board meetings, no board member conversations, nothing.

It took me about two weeks to settle into that and then once I settled in, it was complete bliss. I spent time outside drawing, listening to the birds, waking up with no alarm, watching TV, relaxing, and my creativity began to come back. I began to draw and doodle and write and really think about nothing other than how the silence sounded and what the lilacs looked and smelled like. I would say, "Oh my gosh, look how beautiful my yard is."

I mowed the lawn, sat on the deck, did whatever I wanted, when I wanted and began to detach from the constant conversation in my head about what I did that day, and what I needed to do next.

I have spent 50 years in a constant state of hypervigilance, and that is very unhealthy. I had been in this space since my childhood days of Jake and it was finally taking me down. Halfway into my downtime, we had a tragedy in our family. We lost a young one in a horrific accident, and I was once again reminded that life is too short. I was quickly triggered back into that dark mental space I was all too familiar with.

I was reminded of the fragility of our minds and our lives. I knew if I was not making a conscious and constant effort to be physically healthy and mentally healthy, I would not keep the happiness I had worked so hard to attain. I felt I had no connection to spirituality. I lost the ability to believe in anything outside of myself to get me through this, and in this moment of my life, I felt I was not equipped to get myself through it. I was in an all too familiar space of utter hopelessness, again. There was no way I could even meditate. I couldn't stop the negative and sad thoughts in my head long enough to get any peace of mind.

It was horrible. And again, Alice was there. She listened. She gave me permission to cry. She supported me. She let me know what my value was and that it was essential for me to take time for myself. It was necessary. Nothing, especially Youth Services, was more important than me at that moment in time. In writing this and remembering that space in time only one year ago, I am crying. IT WAS DIFFICULT.

I'm not sure when it occurred to me that the only way for me to move out of this state of mind was to leave the agency. Actually, I do. I do remember now. I was at trauma training and we were in pairs, and I was standing in front of my partner and we were going through an exercise where we stated something that we struggled with. One partner was tasked with directing us to state the reasons we were struggling with an issue. Then other partner was to reply with the questions, "Is it true?" "Is there proof?" The point was to go through the process and get to the bottom of whether it was a true or false belief.

I decided to use the statement, "If I leave Youth Services, it will collapse." My partner played her role perfectly and asked the same question over and over to each one of my responses. I said things like, "I'm the only one that can do the job, not true. I can't teach someone what I do, not true. No one will want the job, not true. I will not find another job, not true. Youth Services will fail if I am not leading it, not true."

AND THAT IS WHEN IT HIT ME. Youth Services will FAIL if I stay in leadership because I cannot do it anymore. I am exhausted. I cannot be objective anymore. I have become the agency. I have no identity anymore. I take things personally, I am emotional, and the list goes on.

In that moment, I burst into hysterical tears. It occurred to me that the only way for Youth Services to remain strong was for me to leave. It was my state of mind that was holding it back from being sustainable. It was like a million light bulbs went on. I just started sobbing and knew I had to move on. So, when I came back, I shared this with Alice, and we became very intentional about what this decision looked like for the future of Youth Services. How would it look for Alice to move into the director position? Do we have a succession plan? How do we make this happen to save my sanity?

During that time of figuring things out, Krissy, one of my friends from ALA, invited me to a virtual women's collective I will call circle, that includes a group call and a one-on-one weekly coaching call. It focuses on women creating abundance in their lives. This sounded perfect because I had recently begun to embrace relationships with women instead of pushing them away. I was feeling supported by women, especially after Alice showed me that strong women can support each other.

The abundance creating part was very inviting and uncomfortable to me as well. And again, just like ALA, it triggered everything in me. My mindset was the usual, I can't. There is no way I can be in this group – a classic conversation around "I'm not worthy. I am not capable of coexisting with the successful women in the group, I am poor Crystal."

I enjoyed my first call, received some incredible coaching from the lead of the circle and decided to choose in. After joining, I was invited into thinking about Dreamweaver on a grander scale. I decided to have a local launch party for Dreamweaver and make the dream boards that I had been talking about online that people were showing interest in. I held the party at one of my favorite restaurants, The Red Pickle, and we filled the restaurant. My friend Mario, the owner, closed the restaurant down and we served appetizers and I led people in my community, which was scary for me, through a dream board session.

There was a large group of people in attendance. I asked a series of questions and people pulled images from magazines, drew images, used quotes and stickers to create a poster of what their dream is. The BIG, even scarier step for this group was to share their dream board amongst people, declare it, increasing the power of the dream. It was incredible to watch people in my community bond, share food, share dreams, and share in the local launch of my dream.

Dream boards have been important in my journey. I made two of them before the launch of Dreamweaver, and have created several since then, so that local launch, along with some other strategies that I implemented, allowed me to declare a departure date from Youth Services.

Launching Dreamweaver locally was something I had not planned to do because it was scary, because it felt easier for me to allow this consulting to live online, to live virtually where I could still be in my community and not really own the fact that I wanted to be a life coach. I was incredibly surprised at the reaction from the community and my friends. People wanted to work with me.

I wanted to see if this was really something I could do. Well of course it was. By that time, we had a team of three at Youth Services in addition to me, which is miraculous, and I decided to take all of them through the Dreamweaver process. There is a two-week process that I used to bond them as new staff members. One word describes the experience for me and them, "Powerful."

We ended up repeating that process towards the end of the succession planning as a way of bonding them as a team with their incoming director, Alice, and I began to see how transformative this work is. My programs were supporting people in making significant life transformations, and that all happened because I chose into the women's circle where I received direct coaching and support to dream bigger.

Alicia Dunams was the lead of circle when I joined, I talk about her in this book because she also created the Bestseller in a Weekend® program that I went through to write this book. One of Alicia's strengths is that she's a strong feminine woman that coaches from her masculine, which is very much what I needed at the time.

During our coaching sessions, I would talk about my plans for Dreamweaver and she would say, "Okay, great. I love it. I love your positive language. When are you going to do this? That lit a fire under me and that's what prompted me to declare my departure date from being director of Youth Services as June 1, 2020. It's scary to declare something big right up until the moment you declare it. Then after you declare it, you realize those are only words, and it wasn't so bad to do it after all.

Immediately my brain started working backwards to put all the steps in place to make June 1st a reality. Yes, it was a made-up deadline that I could move if I wanted to. And in this case, because I knew I needed to move on, Youth Services needed me to move on, and Alice was the one that would be a great director, and, she had two women beside her for a solid team, it was a deadline. I worked with the team and the board to make June 1st a reality. It happened. I left Youth Services, Dreamweaver Consulting lives, I have clients and it is mind-blowing!

I have had the pleasure of working with executive directors and CEOs, in many one-on-one coaching sessions as well as working with nonprofit boards and staff. I created a dynamic process for strategic planning and came up with the *7 Steps to Delivering on Your Dreams* programs that is a four-month process that is changing people's lives. Ideas were literally falling out of me, I was (and still am) on creative fire. The team and I at Youth Services implemented a brilliant succession plan, even during a pandemic and the shelter-in-place mandate. The timing of our transition was, of course, perfect.

During this time, my last child at home, 13-year-old Cooper, and I were really butting heads. What he always came to at the end of our arguments was that he really wanted to live with his father. Now, I am a controller. I did not ever want to let go of that. No way was he going to live with his dad. And after an argument, I asked, "What do you need, because we can't go on like this?"

Cooper responded, "I need to live with my dad."

I was completely shocked to hear the word, "Okay" fall out of my mouth. It was Christmas break, 2019 and after I realized what I said, in my mind, I thought, okay, he can go stay with his father during Christmas break. That will be good; he will get it out of his system. Well, little did I know that "accidentally" letting go of that control and letting him live with his dad, was leading him to getting happier and he and his dad are doing great. This is an incredible gift.

Despite the difficulty of letting go of control of my youngest child, it was beautiful to witness. Letting go led to an incredible chain of events, that started on a day when I was meeting with the CEO of the Local Chamber of Commerce, Amy, a current client. I said, "If I could find an apartment downtown, (we live in a beautiful rural county) I would sell my house and move. I want an upstairs place, overlooking downtown, the city center of Ellensburg."

She responded, "Oh yeah, I've always wanted to live downtown." The very next week, this is 100% true, the very next week, we were sitting in her office and she's said, "I was going to ask you if you saw that apartment downtown for rent?" I was like, "what?" She was like, "yeah." So, she pulled it up on her computer, and there it was. I could cry thinking about it right now, this beautiful one bedroom, kitchen, bathroom, living room, (you know, small apartment yet big enough), overlooking downtown Ellensburg, brick accent walls, wood floor. Incredible.

I declared out loud, "I get to have that." Now mind you, I was still living in my home that I had bought through this incredible, dream, declare, deliver process. Living there I would often have moments when I drove down that street on the way home, and I would think, I can't believe it. That is my house. I bought that by myself. Hot tub, beautiful backyard. You name it.

And now I am thinking, this is it. This is my dream apartment. This is what I asked for. Oh my gosh, this dream, declare, deliver manifestation stuff really works. I desperately wanted this apartment and when I viewed it in person, I knew it had to be mine. The lady who owns the apartment building was busy and I hounded her, letting her know how excited I was to live in this apartment. Of course, I got the apartment and within two weeks of getting the apartment, I had completely emptied my house, downsized a three-bedroom, two-bathroom house into a one-bedroom, one-bathroom apartment. I moved, set it up perfectly in two days, and listed my house for sale by owner on the market. Crazy! People thought, what the heck is she doing?!

I sat down one night and thought, what have I done? I had all the conversations with Cooper and his father. They decided that they were solid and were going to stick with the living arrangement for the next five years. They were fine with mom getting an apartment. There'd be enough room for Cooper to visit anytime, he would get to stay in his school, and the apartment was only seven miles away.

Within one month of saying I wanted to move, I was in my dream apartment.

Being stubborn and aware that this was my only investment, I wanted to sell my house myself, so that's how I listed it. I ended up having a realtor friend support me in selling the house. It turned out to be quite a ride with lots of "trusting the process" moments, especially when the pandemic hit. I declared on a Monday that we were going to sell my house that week, and we had a cash offer on that following Monday. That same week on Friday we closed the deal, and the money was in the bank. I was thinking to myself, oh my gosh, I'm even blowing my own self away. That is manifestation!

How freaking intense. Declaring what you want is how to start the law of attraction process. Trusting the process is essential. When you ask the universe, God, whatever you want to call it, for something, believe in it, work for it, you get it. AND it will come to you in the way that it is supposed to, for your greatest good.

Fast forward to March 2020, I was in a beautiful location to shelter in place, and happy. There are four windows that look out over downtown just as I had declared. This book was born in this apartment. This is the place where the poetry that you can read in future books was chosen from my files. I wept for hours reading that poetry, realizing that as far back as 1993, I had been dreaming, declaring, and delivering. I have been making incredible things happen and I sometimes question how I did it. I did it all with the 7 Steps that you just read and are available to anyone. Just a couple of days ago, my client, Marlene, said something to me. Her statement will bring this chapter to a perfect close and lead into the next chapter, where my four friends (to include Marlene) and former clients talk about their peer reading experience of the book.

Marlene said, "Oh my gosh, I've been trying to figure out why it is so powerful to lose my victim mindset? What is that about?

"I was looking at your website and I read your mission statement, that 'only with a victim-free mindset and feeling worthy can we choose the life of our dreams.'"

My reply was, "Yes." I knew the words of my mission were the right words and yet they didn't land in my heart the way they landed when Marlene said, "ONLY with the victim-free mindset and feeling worthy, can I choose my life." I replied to Marlene, "Wow, that is BIG, and I created that. I created Dreamweaver Consulting. That is me. That is Crystal, that is Chief Dreamweaver."

To clarify, the above statement is me living my purpose of lifting people up. That is not me being tied to the ego of, I did create it. It is the fire in my soul to listen to people like Marlene have these profound aha moments and support them through the breakdowns that lead to a breakthrough.

You will hear these victory stories in the next chapter from the four ladies. The chapter with my adult children will be the story of breaking cycles. You are in for a treat. The most satisfying conversation to date, between my daughter, oldest son, and myself. So, thank you from the bottom of my heart for joining me on this freaking amazing journey. And if you feel a connection with me, we get to work together because I am telling you, this process will blow your mind, *you* will blow your mind.

FEEDBACK

This conversation was held over a Zoom meeting with those four ladies I mentioned in earlier chapters, who graciously read my rough draft manuscript with the intent to give me feedback. The feedback was incredible, and I wanted to capture it "live." What you will read is a condensed version of our conversation.

Crystal: All right. We are all here. I'm super excited and I thought it would be cool to start by talking about how you are connected to me. Let's start by sharing your "I am" statement and what it means to you. Reality, you get to go first. Then we will go Alice, Ori, and Marlene! The fabulous foursome.

Reality: I am Reality and I am a fun, caring, adventurous woman. To me, my "I am" statement has meant something different every day of my journey. Most recently it has meant something that I feel comfortable to embrace daily and live up to. (For readers who are wondering what the "I am" statement is, it is your mantra, or your spirit contract, or the words you feel describe you.)

Crystal: Oh, I love that. I am also going to talk about how I know each of you. I met Reality because she walked into the Community

Network and she said, "Hi, I'm Reality and I want to be an intern." She proceeded to tell me all about her major at Central Washington University and I shared the new mentor program I was creating. For the next hour we talked and laughed and cried and the rest is history. She was literally the muscle behind ripping out the carpet with me, hammering down nails, cleaning on our hands and knees, and whatever else it took to get the physical space welcoming. She created the first logo. We had an instant connection. I remember feeling something similar with each one of you. Each of our connections have unique qualities as well.

Alice: Reality, I have to say it is an honor to finally meet you because I've heard so much about you.

Reality: "Oh, it's nice to see you too, Alice".

Alice: I am Alice Nelson, and I am a caring, courageous, and powerful woman. And that is a huge proclamation for me because those are things that in my past, I haven't always felt that I was, and that other people may have made me feel like I wasn't. Now I get to own it. It is freeing when you finally own it.

Crystal: Awesome. I love it. I met Alice on a car ride to Yakima, Washington, when we went to an Adverse Childhood Experiences Study (ACEs) training together. At that time, she was working in a community partner agency. We talked openly and naturally all the way there and back, and in my mind I thought I had just found the next director of Youth Services. I need this woman in my professional life.

We continued to meet for coffee and create a friendship. I shared with her my desire to have her on the Youth Services team. I was clear that as soon as possible I would be coming back to her and offering her a job. I wrote a successful state grant that created an open position. I went back to her, let her know about the opening, clearly attempting to poach her from the other agency. She almost didn't apply, and I called her and encouraged her to apply. I said, "What are you doing? I created this job description with you in mind!"

And then I had to step back and let the board interview everyone, and they picked her. Thank God. If not, I was fully prepared to override their decision on the grounds that I needed this woman in my professional circle. Right now, during this Zoom meeting, Alice is exactly 23 days away from becoming the Director of Youth Services and has been working in the co-director position for almost six months. That is a huge amount of learning and work in little time. Awesome job Alice. Okay, Ori, you get to go next.

Ori: I am Ori, and my "I am" statement started out as I am an intuitive, caring, beautiful woman, and along the way it changed to, "I'm an intuitive, caring, beautiful healer." And I really think that is what it means to me. I have been able to embrace and own that I am a healer and Crystal has helped to bring that out. Now I can share it with the world. It has been awesome.

Crystal: Ori lives in the same community as I do. I have received healing services from her and taken her yoga classes. One day we were talking and I shared that I was in long term recovery and that Alcoholics Anonymous (AA) wasn't my thing in long-term sobriety and I wanted to create this Dreamweaver thing that would reach all people to include people in recovery. And so, between the two of us talking, that's how the expansion of the program beyond 2-weeks got its start. Ori and I had a soul connection, a healer to healer connection immediately. Then, one day when we were talking, we learned we *freaking* have the same birthday! Like seriously, both of us were born on May 7th.

Marlene my friend, you are next.

Marlene: Yes. I am Marlene. I am a sober, committed, courageous, and loving woman. And it did not start off like that. I changed it on April 1st when I "Chose In." I am committed to finishing things that I start now. I haven't always been. I've always quit and I'm courageous for stepping out of fear and using my voice to be heard. I have always been loving.

Crystal: Marlene and I walked into a San Diego Hotel to attend the same Ascension Leadership Academy (ALA), transformation session. We landed in the first small group together and bonded. This bond increased as we went through the most impactful transformation of our lives together. The loving part of Marlene is why we connected on a deeper level. As a strong female when a loving female steps in and nurtures me in a way that I can receive, it is profound. Marlene did this, and we are bonded for life. Marlene is a gentle and loving woman. Most recently, Marlene used her voice to stand up to me in a difficult coaching conversation. She owned her voice and said, "I don't feel like you're hearing me." That moment was monumental, unforgettable, and gave Marlene the power of her voice back. She took her power back!

I did not realize until I started to gather you ladies, that you've all been through the Dreamweaver process. I really did not. I just knew that you four were the people I trusted completely with this vulnerable information.

As I am looking at the Zoom screen, I see women who are leaders and I'm super excited to hear the book feedback from all of you. I've never written anything as vulnerable as this book. My whole life has been leading up to the writing of this book. I had no idea it was ready to come out of me until the day it came out. The story has a life all its own. I know this book is the platform that I get to freaking launch from and it's exciting. I'm going to leave the rest up to you four, and if you have questions, comments, we have 20 minutes or so slated for our conversation about *"The Evolution of Dreamweaver: 7 Steps for Delivering on Your Dreams."*

Reality: Life Coaching was not anything I had ever considered or investigated. So, when I texted you and I said, I'm freaking lost, I don't understand what's happening in my life. I don't know where I'm going, and I hate this feeling. What are your suggestions? And you said, you are in my program. That is what the suggestions are. We are doing it. Hearing you say this was scary. I didn't understand what life coaching was, but it's been a big turning point in my life, and I can't tell people about it enough. When I'm talking to my friends, when I'm making videos, when I'm talking to my family, I just want to share this resource that I didn't know existed. I did not know I needed it, and I didn't know it could help me. It has been exactly what I need and at the exact time that I need it. Thank you.

Crystal: It has happened exactly as it was supposed to. And I think we're all going to feel emotional on this Zoom because, this is one of those profound moments in time where the conversation is a real, raw and unscripted conversation about the impact of this book on you. The book is my story, the story of Crystal Church, Chief Dreamweaver, and Jake.

Ori: I feel exactly the same way, Reality. I did not ever consider life coaching and it was top notch and it has changed my life so much. My whole life is completely different. It's a life changing process. I never knew that it could be like this.

Marlene: I would not have even imagined how good my life after the Dreamweaver process would be. Yeah. You know? Yes, and it all starts with the victim-free mindset.

Alice: I resonate with your comments and what's interesting for me is that I have had the opportunity to walk alongside Crystal this whole time Dreamweaver has been unfolding. I was working with Crystal at Youth Services and got to be there from the start of her dreaming the idea of Dreamweaver. We would always have conversations because she was my boss, and then she would life coach me in the middle of work, you know, because that's just who she is. Boss or not, and she couldn't stop being Dreamweaver and life coaching me. It is how she lives. And that is the thing that resonated with me from the book. It was insightful being able to work beside you during the time you started Dreamweaver, as well as when you started writing this book. I was watching you create a safe space for me to step into the new me.

I think that is what life coaching is about. And that is what Crystal is about, walking the walk. I love that Crystal would always tell me, own your story. I did not always want to hear that, and she'd call me forth all the time. She is someone who has also experienced trauma and has experienced the struggle. Anyone who ends up reading the book, whether they've experienced trauma or not, they will relate to it because everyone's experienced some kind of struggle and it's about owning it, talking about it, and creating space for people to live it out. Space to reflect on it and become who they are meant to be. I think for me this book was just a perfect next chapter to me knowing you, Crystal, because it was inspiring watching you teach me all these tools along the way and mentor me as I practiced them. Now I get to step into the role of director at Youth Services, as I watch you literally share your story at the biggest level ever. Sharing my story is exactly what you've been encouraging me to do, and here you are doing it now. This book creates a safe space for me to share my story in my own way. It is incredible to have another woman setting that example by walking the walk and talking talk.

Crystal: We are the future. And I do not mean that in a sexist way. We are the future. We (women) have a different mindset, a different way of looking at things. And if men are reading this book, this doesn't mean that you're not valuable. It means let us embrace the partnership in life and let's be open to others' ways of thinking. Women bring a whole different yin to the yang. The thing that brings me the most joy is that I have cried in front of all of you, I have snotty-cried, and that is where the growth is for me, in being vulnerable. Vulnerability is a big word because my lady Brené Brown made it big. (By the way, she is going to read this book and endorse it eventually). It is true that when you can be human, people can identify with you.

Because everybody has read the story of Jake and Crystal at this point, it's okay to talk about the paralleling stories. These two stories are the basis of the book and were written in two days. I had the skeleton of the book in my mind for years, and an idea of how I wanted the story to flow, and when I began writing it downloaded out of me in two days. I say "downloaded" because that is what it felt like. I was speaking into zoom and my hands were typing all my life experiences into a story that felt guided. I was not sure if there would be confusion about Crystal, Dreamweaver, and Jake. I wasn't sure how to tell my story in a way that if my parents pick it up and read it, they don't hate me, and yet I couldn't lie either; it is my story. I'd love to hear how that played out for you in your mind.

Ori: I feel like you gave your mom more grace than I might have given my mom. I recall thinking Crystal's got a lot of grace in there.

Crystal: That is why the book didn't come out until now. And I can honestly say that coaching other people and seeing the power that anger had over people, helped me move through that.

Marlene: I thought it was easy to read and there was no confusion. You wove the two together, and it was perfect. While I was reading it, at first, I didn't know you and Jake were the same person.

I loved the fact that you had your grandma in your life, and I think if everybody had somebody like that for support, it would be life altering. I could feel that love you have for her.

Ori: Me too, Marlene, when I read the introduction, I texted Crystal and I said, is Lucas real? Because I have never met a man like that in my life, seriously! I totally had goosebumps when I read that part because it was like, I mean, I knew he was real, but it was simply crazy. Before, when we were talking about powerful women and you said, "we are the future," I think that we will help men become more like Lucas and help them be more open and, and that's part of the future too.

Crystal: Yes, he does exist. And there were so many good little bits of wisdom in that introduction.

What about you, Alice? Reality?

Reality: As I read through, I noticed my ego speaking to me a bit and I noticed myself making comparisons to my own life. I realize that just because we haven't been through the same trauma doesn't mean that trauma hasn't affected us in similar ways. It doesn't mean that we haven't all hurt from something, because I think everyone has been hurt by something. That was a strong thought that I had to stop and think more about. Also, when I was reading, I thought about the acknowledgements, like Ori was saying, when you were talking about your parents and saying they did the best they could with the tools that they had. It made me consider, gosh, if I wrote about my life, who would I be hurting? Would I be affecting people? Would people think I was lying? Would they think that my story wasn't true? You told so much in your book, it was vulnerable.

Alice: Reading this book causes reflection of your own story. It causes the reader to reflect on what Jake's going through before you get to the end. You do a comparison and then self-reflection. I don't know many books off the top of my head that have ever caused that kind of reaction for me, to actually be able to relate in such a close way that I immediately start to reflect, and ask myself how do I judge others in different situations? Or how do I judge my own story? This book is clearly showing me that I'm judgmental of my own self and that needs to stop.

This book makes the reader want to share their own story. The book is empowering and triggers a chain reaction of vulnerability. One person shares, and then the next person. Now it's two people, and then before you know it is a movement of women owning their stories. Learning to embrace your story and look at the opportunities and gifts is how change is created. This book gives the reader permission to dream your dreams and act on them. It is life changing.

Ori: When I went through the two-week program, you taught me to own my story and I did. I did and my husband told me what I was feeling was wrong. I decided to get a divorce because that's my story and you can't tell me not to feel what I feel.

Crystal: And so, then the next day in coaching, she starts with "Hi, I'm Ori, and oh, by the way, I'm getting a divorce." I didn't even know what to say. I had all these feelings of like, oh my God, what have you done, Crystal? I did my best to listen to Ori and not my inner dialogue. Ori assured me, "No, this is good." Within a couple of months, Ori purchased a place, worked as a team with her soon to be ex-husband to remodel it, paint, furnish it beautifully, and move herself and her children into her sanctuary of peace. Ori is a woman on a mission to find happiness, freaking amazing.

Ori: It is because of Dreamweaver. I was able to own my story and voice it with respect to myself. I started the full life transformation version of the Dreamweaver process the week after I moved, and I have been able to uncover many layers of myself. Realizations and thoughts keep coming and I have been able to sit down and see what my authentic life is. I see who I am and started down that path of authenticity. Therefore, I say there are not enough words to describe what you do. I now see what I can do with my life.

Crystal: I am proud to know all of you. I love the menagerie of ages and personalities gathered on this Zoom. I am excited at the thought of each and every one of you moving forward as your best selves.

Alice: There is this weird thing that happens when you break cycles, that you coached me through, Crystal. People in your life make you feel like you are wrong for being healthy and changing your life, and they put you down. It is hard not to believe it. I would think I am doing something wrong, when really it is them who haven't shifted yet. Crystal, you encouraged me to keep going. You would say, "They'll shift, don't worry, keep living it out. You are living your story, Alice, and they will follow, or they will fall away." I remember we would have calls and you would say, "Do you realize what just happened Alice? You are setting the example of what healthy boundaries and reactions look like. Do you see what you're teaching your young daughter?"

This is what is important about your book. You are showing the shift in Jake's story and you're showing how when you stick with it you shift, despite what anyone else thinks. If you stick with it, you will reach the outcome. Look at where you are now, Crystal, and what you have accomplished. Hearing these testimonials from other people is inspiring. There are so many women who are stuck in these unhealthy, toxic relationships where they feel like they have no options. It is stories like yours in the book that could help countless women in domestic violence situations. I get goosebumps listening to all the feedback. It is intense.

Crystal: This conversation reminds me of the book, "Hillbilly Elegy." The author of Hillbilly Elegy, J. D. Vance, talks about his life in the South and how he broke multiple cycles of abuse, from physical abuse to substance abuse and addiction. His family didn't want to see him grow because it made them uncomfortable. He went to Harvard and became a lawyer and always felt like himself as a kid when he went back home. It was a struggle to break free from the Hillbilly Elegy. I loved how his Grandma, Maw Maw, in the story, was his person just like my Grandma.

Alice and I would use the term "Hillbilly Elegy" in our conversation to skip a long drawn out explanation of our childhoods. It always brought a smile to our faces and a giggle. Speaking of cycle breaking, I remembered at 23 years old, after the birth of my first child, Alex, the incredibly detailed memories of what had happened to me as a child. I'm never going to lie to anyone and say this process of healing was easy, because I'm 52 years old and this has spanned almost 30 years. I know it is always going to be a story that is evolving and unfolding. The difference at 52 is that I am not afraid of it. I embrace it; it makes me strong. I'm excited to hear Alex's feedback on the book because she's this living human testament to the entire journey. She has been there since my first memory of my childhood trauma.

Speaking of my daughter, Alex, she texted me today and made a big decision and wanted to thank me for supporting her through it. It was in that moment when I realized that when your own child sees the value of your words, it's freaking phenomenal.

"Ori and Alice, Savannah's five, right? And Dacoda's five?" These two little girls will never walk the paths that any of us walked. Because you are intentional in your mothering and it's never, ever too late to make changes. Our kids always are so proud of us when we make the shifts that they may never tell us they wish we would, but they do wish it deep inside.

Reality: I found my favorite part of the book was all the times in which I could hear your voice and there was a lot of times where your voice really rang through in your writing. And I think that's important because it allows people, even people that have only met you once, or people that you've talked to on the phone, or people that don't know you, hear the real you. There is going to be something in there where they hear you and they relate. There are so many times in the book where you made me giggle, and picture you. I felt personally connected to the book. People will hear that you are a real person, fricking sassy as heck, funny, and charismatic.

Crystal: I love it. I am excited to do a book tour, so people get to see me and hear me talk about the book. This will support them in hearing "me" in it when they read it.

Reality: Your vulnerability is unheard of, when you share it's like the reader almost knows you, even if you have never met in your life. Readers will feel that connection, it is your energy. You feel that intensity and it empowers you as a reader to make your own changes and to weave your own dreams.

Crystal: Weave your own dreams, mic drop.

Marlene: I loved it. And I'm looking forward to reading your book of poetry when it comes out.

Crystal: That is right! The poetry. Yes. That was another whole journey. Right after I wrote this story; it was literally 11:00 o'clock at night, and I was in my apartment crying, cheering because I have just given birth to this ginormous part of me. Waiting for everybody to read it was painful, so I needed to occupy my time. I thought I was going to put some of my artwork in it, so I dug out a file of what I thought was artwork that turned out to be poetry. Some of it is poetry written when I was out of my mind on drugs and alcohol and it is still beautiful. My thoughts were (and still are) amazing!

I am blown away how I knew how to dream, declare, and deliver back then. Reading it made me cry because in so much of the poetry, I was literally fighting to live. The poetry speaks to this relationship I had with suicide my whole life. The underlying theme of most of the poetry is, do not give up. It was like the two sides of me, the strong side, and the weak broken side, talking to each other in the poetry and pushing me through it. Those words made me weep and sad for that time in my life. The poems about never giving up on your dreams were crazy foreshadowing for what was going to evolve in 2019 – Dreamweaver Consulting. It is the supporting documentation of my journey. I'm excited to create a coffee table book with pictures of the poems, because some of them are written on random things from wherever I was. Some of the poetry you can tell how messed up and wasted I am simply by the handwriting. Thanks Marlene.

Marlene: I love the idea of the picture of the original because it is raw, that makes me want to cry, too.

Crystal: I am super excited for this entire process. I love that I have decided that the book gets to end the same way it started with a Zoom conversation with the people who mean the world to me. Then when I'm doing my audiobook, like David Goggins, "Can't Hurt Me: Master Your Mind and Defy the Odds," someone will read it and then we'll stop at each chapter and talk in between … this conversation with the four of you high-powered ladies lives near the end. We get to be famous together. Famous because of your own stories.

Marlene: You have given permission for people to own their story. You've given me permission.

Crystal: All of you have a beautiful story and I cannot wait to read every one of them. Your story matters and makes a difference.

Reality: Crystal, you said that, and all of us nodded at the same time. I know that a lot of people are scared to tell their story because the people who caused the trauma have told them they can't tell their story or told them that their story isn't real and that it's all in their head. And it helps to realize that you can tell your story. You don't have to be afraid and you're not crazy. It's your story.

Crystal: I can relate to what you said Reality. When I was 23, and I had Alex and I took the video about incest that I created in college and gave it to each side of my family. It felt like the little town where I grew up was split completely in half. You had the camp that could not imagine this happened and believed that my father's side of the story was the truth. Then you had the camp that was my mom's side that said they believed me, and then me in the middle where I felt like nobody believed me and that I was crazy. If I would not have gone to counseling to validate the signs and symptoms of the effects of this childhood abuse, I wouldn't have believed me either. It is an earth shattering feeling when you look up incest and domestic violence trauma and the definition is your life.

After I wrote this book, my throat closed off when I thought about what I had done. That whole visceral reaction of "you shouldn't have done that. You have done something wrong." And then, when it took people a long time to read, I was totally in my head about it. In my mind I was saying, oh my God they think it's horrible. It is offensive, it's too much. That dialogue was so loud, I was not able to realize that everybody has their own life and they will read it when they can. I had the same internal reaction with waiting for my daughter to read it. It took her the longest of anybody to read it and she was the one that I needed to read it first, and I got to wait and be patient. I got to trust the process. I got to utilize the delay. Through this part of the book process, I learned everybody is going to have their own reaction.

Reality: And each person's reaction is because of their own story and how they relate to your story. My story, the Reality story impacts what I get out of your story, as with everything, right?

Alice: I think about my time in the military; eight percent of the Marine Corps is female, so I mostly worked with men, and when I was experiencing certain things and I'd have guys say things like, "She is just crazy," I now understand it's because they can't relate to our female experience.

What is cool about this book is, it explains your journey in a way that all people can stop and self-reflect. Anyone can, even those who have not experienced what you have, and who tend to judge and jump to conclusions. People will be able to self-reflect and say, "Wow, this person went through all of this. Those are things I typically see in other people that I would call them crazy, because of X, Y, Z and maybe I should start thinking a little bit more before I just immediately jump to conclusions about people in my life or people that I interact with."

Crystal: Alice, you just made me think of something that I didn't even plan with the two versions of my story. My actual story as Crystal, Chief Dreamweaver is the light side of things, the normal-ish challenges we all go through. The fairy tale success story is, if we dream, declare, deliver, we can still make it through and crush our goals. Intentionally using Jake's story to describe the extreme trauma version of dreaming, declaring, and delivering allows people to see that this life path also leads to crushing dreams. The twist at the end is when I take readers, who believed Crystal and Jake to be two separate people with two separate lives and merge them into the same person. Spotlighting that dreaming, declaring, and delivering is available to everyone! Does not matter which person in the story you related to in the end because they are the same person. Mic drop on judgement.

Reality: Every coaching call that I had with you, just like this Zoom conversation, made me realize something profound in myself and my own life. When you were talking, Alice, about people thinking something is crazy because they don't understand, that is something that I do with my partner all the time and I never recognized what it was. The truth is that I did not understand what he was talking about.

And now I am like, shoot, now we have to talk about it tonight. Correction, we get to talk about it tonight. I never even knew until this moment that is what was happening. Thank you for saying all those things and helping me realize something that I get to talk about with my partner.

Crystal: I want to thank you all for your wisdom. You have reinforced that it's okay to mess things up, that we are human and do make mistakes. We judge others, and sometimes are self-critical, and that's human nature and it's part of life; it is out of survival. You must be able to look at someone and say, is this a threat or is this a safe place for me? It is literally hardwired into who we are at a chemical level and we get to let go of the judgment, the self-judgment for that, as well.

Alice: I learned something. If you can start catching yourself in those moments or even after, that is what matters. That is what Dreamweaver teaches – that place between, where you can pause and see it. I have noticed that since going through Dreamweaver more than once with you Crystal, I would recognize things in myself quicker and quicker and it just took practice. It is hard-wiring your brain to recognize, like you always tell me, what are you feeling in your body right now? Or you would ask, when you were experiencing that, what were you feeling? You asked this to teach me to recognize it before it happens or in the moment and then shift. Another thing that's impactful about Dreamweaver is having someone to hold you accountable and be on the outside looking in and ask the questions that allow you to see it yourself.

Crystal: You have completed the 2-week program I have created, the Dreamweaver Full Life Transformation program, which is most beneficial for a full life transformation. The two-week, unless you are highly evolved, is not enough. It has the potential to leave you at a point where it is easy to backslide. It was perfect that we worked together more than once, Alice.

Ori: I'm focusing on my recovery from alcohol as part of the Dreamweaver Full Life Transformation program, and I have shared with Crystal, it would be a great tool to show progress for a person in early recovery to go through it and then go through it again in a year because you're going to get so many more layers the second time around.

Crystal: All of you have played such a huge part in my journey, your feedback and trust in me has been incredible. This conversation for example is so rich and from the space of being in the flow of a great conversation. It has been fun to see where the conversation has taken us. I love you all. Seriously, from the bottom of my heart. I am excited for you all to see the next version of it, where my adult children share their story of reading the book and growing up with Crystal, Jake, and Chief Dreamweaver as their mom. It will prove to be insightful, and proof that cycles of abuse of all kinds can be stopped. I love you all. Have a great night. Bye for now.

THE GIFT OF BROKEN CYCLES

W ell, we have made to the most important chapter of all. The chapter that defines my favorite quote, "be the change."

The following summary of the Zoom call with my kids was "take two" for us. The first interview was beautiful, vulnerable and unlike any conversation I have ever had with two of my children. I am proud of these two and honored they were willing to be part of the grand finale of the book. They are a product of my hard work breaking generational cycles of abuse and addiction. They are the next generation who lead lives free from my chains of trauma that weighed me down.

Okay, here we go, the long-awaited Dreamweaver discussion from two of the most important humans in my life, Alexandra Elizabeth, and Tyler James.

Crystal: Let's start this process because I've been thinking about it all day. We had a heart-warming Zoom last night. I was so touched, and I was crying because it was one of those moments where the things you guys said to me where things I never dreamed I would hear. And so, hearing how you really liked me was touching, and then to find out it didn't record, I lost my mind.

I was in complete breakdown. Alex assured me it was okay. I kept saying, no it is not. I wanted to listen to that conversation again, over and over. I wanted to have those words saved. Then I went completely off the deep end and said that I did not even want to write the book anymore.

Alex and Tyler's role in life has been to figure out what their mom was freaking out about. When anxiety sets in, the whole world flies apart. Everything sucks. Thank you, Tyler, and Alex, for talking me off the ledge and making sure this chapter got done, and I finish this book.

Tyler and Alex, what do you want the readers to know about each of you?

Tyler: I am 21 years old, middle child of Chief Dreamweaver.

Crystal: Man of many words. (The three of us laugh!)

Alex: I am Alex. I am the oldest child, the only girl, and I live in Ellensburg where I have spent most of my time. I did live in Arizona for a little bit and on the west side of the mountains, Seattle area, and currently I am back at home in Ellensburg. I am 28.

Crystal: What do you want readers to know about Chief Dreamweaver Crystal Church?

Alex: What I want people to know about Chief Dreamweaver is she is a mom first and that is important.

Tyler: Like Alex said, she is first mom, our mom, mother to three of us. That has always been a priority in life, and Chief Dreamweaver has also always been there too.

I think I have always seen you as mom, and it's been interesting to see your growth as you became involved in more things than just being my mom. Right now, you are Chief Dreamweaver and before that you were head of Youth Services. It has been cool to watch you transition.

A big thing is having the courage and the strength to share Chief Dreamweaver with the world. You have always shared with the world that you're a mom, and whether people realize it, you've always been Chief Dreamweaver, too. The difference now is that you have written a book and started a consultancy to share that with the rest of the world.

Crystal: It reminds me of the first time I read it on the website. I thought that's kind of weird. Am I going to introduce myself as Chief Dreamweaver? It started out kind of as a joke. And then I remember I was at the Kittitas County Chamber of Commerce leading this strategic planning process, and we were done, and someone said, "Hey, Chief Dreamweaver," and proceeded to ask me a question. I decided in that moment to step into this and act "as if." And now I say it all the time! I own it!

What do you want the readers to know about your mom?

Alex: I have always seen the Chief Dreamweaver characteristic in you; and there's a difference between my mom and Chief Dreamweaver. The difference when you're being mom versus the Chief Dreamweaver is a level of professionalism. There's the same underlying compassion, but I definitely see a difference on the mom level type of things. Not that they cannot go side-by-side, but if I am wanting to have a mom conversation, it's just a mom conversation.

Tyler: For me, I want people to know that it comes down to me allowing myself to overcome the defensiveness that comes up for me, more than anything. I must work on letting it be okay to take advice or direction from someone else, Chief Dreamweaver and separate her from my mom.

Crystal: Hearing that you each were resisting coaching because I'm your mom AND I'm a transformation life coach, I can see where it would be difficult at certain ages to take my advice or my guidance. Difficult to see the coaching side of me. I interpreted it as you didn't think I could do it (be a life coach) and you didn't think it was a good idea; you didn't think it was cool. This fed my old story of being worried about what people think. That has been a huge part of my growth and personal development. And, finally, I decided to keep plugging along and trust you two would come around.

Your feedback is valuable because it's teaching me to be completely objective for you when you are requesting coaching, versus requesting the mom version of me. I can recognize now that I set extremely high standards for the two of you. I remember Tyler saying at one point during high school, "You do not even know how hard it is to be your kid: every year you have to do everything to the highest of your ability."

Alex: I think I felt like you held me to a double standard for a long time. You didn't want me to make these mistakes or take these certain paths because it is what you did, but because you did all these things, I felt you should understand. That is where I always felt like the life coach aspect of you was hard. Transitioning between mom and life coach was tough.

Crystal: I can see that. I feel like the Chief Dreamweaver side of me can be more compassionate. The mom side of me was so worried about you two following my path that my thought was always, no, you will do better. I remember saying to each of you, I know you are trying, but try harder. You are so smart, and you can do better. Now I understand that's not always supportive. The next question references the sentence that reads, "My father used to call me Jake when I was a kid." What was your reaction to Jake's story?

Alex: I thought reading the book that I would be sad or have lots of emotions that maybe I was not expecting, but I was empowered and proud of you and happy. Happy to see that you shared your story. I was not sad, which kind of shocked me. I didn't feel sorrow, not that I don't have compassion for what you've been through, but it was more an overwhelming sense of pride that you were strong and courageous enough to get your story out and share it with people.

This book is huge and something I know that you wanted to do for a long time. I was proud because I know it was not an easy step to take. You delivered the book effectively and people are going to hear your story and grow from it and relate to it more than anything else.

Crystal: Writing this book has been a catharsis.

Alex: The book has been a process for us kids, too. Since reading the book, the three of us, (you, me and Tyler) have expressed things that we haven't ever expressed before. The first Zoom that wasn't recorded isn't part of your story and that's for something to come later. Those are chapters of another book.

Crystal: In hindsight Alex, I can see that. But when you said to me, "Maybe there's a gift in it not recording," I thought in my head really like, really? You are going to freaking coach me right now while I'm in breakdown. You were right; it was a special moment that it gets to stay ours.

Tyler: When I heard it did not record and you didn't want to do it again, I was saying, "Buck up sister." I think me and Alex went through the same inner dialogue, it didn't record. Well isn't that just great, we just are going to have to do this all over again. You know? And then Alex called me and was saying exactly what I was thinking. That was kind of a growth moment by itself. We got to reaffirm with everyone that we were still in this, we are still doing it, you know.

Crystal: I felt nurtured and loved when Alex said, "Mom, it'll be okay. We'll just do it again." And, of course, my inner sass was also saying, "I am really irritated that you're going to be the voice of reason with me right now".

Alex: You didn't want that voice of reason. You wanted me to be that person to get you riled back up and I didn't. I said we would do it over.

Tyler: No one ever wants to hear the voice of reason. The voice of reason is always the dickhead who is right when you're wrong.

Crystal: Ha ha ha. So, what was your reaction to Jake's story Ty?

Tyler: I thought it was a very satisfying end to the story on an emotional level. You were alluding to you being Jake about halfway through the story. You sort of dropped the hint that it was you. I remember you mentioned to me that you wrote the story this way because you wanted to elicit a certain emotional response from the reader, and I think that was effective. It made the conclusion of the story feel like you were trying to tell the story because it was necessary to show your growth, not because you wanted to show how much of a victim you were.

Crystal: Next question: What was it like having Jake as a parent? Someone parenting from a traumatic background like your mom.

Tyler: It came with its challenges. There were parts that were hard because of the substance abuse and because of whatever else was going on at the time. I think that every childhood is going to have some challenges. And I think the challenges we experienced probably served us well in a lot of the cases. I do not think we had an ideal upbringing by any means, but what is an ideal upbringing? And if you can expose kids to things early, I think it is good in a lot of cases. And I think we got a lot of that, whether it was on purpose or not, you know?

Alex: In the conversations that we've had, it's interesting to compare our outlooks. Obviously, Cooper's not at the age where he can quite understand or share these things, however we all three had a vastly different upbringing. The same mom, and each of us have a different view on our childhood or upbringing or opinion of how we were raised. We will always have similarities and it is interesting to see how each one of them differs. For me, I think it is the transparency that you had with me as a child. I am grateful for that. I experienced things that a lot of kids probably never have. And it shaped how I look at the world, gave me my unique perspective. And like Tyler said, you know, there were challenges, but it made us the people that we are today.

Crystal: You two are amazing humans. When Alex was born, I was fully engulfed in addiction. I got sober when Tyler was seven, when I was pregnant with Cooper. You have all seen me in a varying degree of addiction. It makes sense that you were parented differently, at the same time with the same essence of the human that I am. The people I met and the places we traveled together had a different impact on each of us lending to our individual perspective.

Alex: That is the chapter for a future book that I was talking about, the chapter that doesn't exist in this book. It includes those special things that we have never talked about before. I'm 28 and I have never had conversations about some of those things that have occurred in my past. And when we talked about them yesterday, our upbringing and what it was like growing up with you experiencing the trials and tribulations, it occurred to me that it brought many people into our lives that we may not have otherwise had.

We had many different support systems, and that showed us that you can rely on more than one person. It's like a tribe raising a family, which is what we had. We had these people who would pick us up when we needed picked up. There were babysitters, and if I didn't want to go home, I had a best friend whose parents would let me stay for a week if I wanted. If we didn't have money to buy certain things, they stepped up. I appreciate people in a different light, and it makes me want to give back to people. That generosity is instilled in me and I want to help other people who are less fortunate, no matter what, and I love that about myself; it is a great quality.

Crystal: Alex you said something that I have never heard before. That was so cool. A tribe raising a family.

I can reflect and see that I did not have all the tools necessary to parent. I was in a fight or flight mode most of the formative years of all three of your childhoods. I agree that the tribe raising the family was crucial to our journey. Maybe that is also another book co-written by you and me, Alex? That would be incredible.

Alex: Perfect and we talked about how those people are still in our lives. You have come a long way. You may not need the support from the tribe in the same way as before. It is not the same aspect of raising your children, and yet they're still support systems. They are important people who want to be a part of those big milestones in our lives, support us, and are proud to see how far you've come, Mom. Our tribe is proud of how far we've come along in our growing up; they want to know what we're doing in our lives. That is pretty cool.

Crystal: Anything else about what it was like having Jake as Mom?

Tyler: No, I think I got out what I was trying to say about hard knocks.

Alex: It is hard. I think it is difficult to say I had a hard childhood. Some crazy things happened for me. I don't ever want to say that it was difficult, because I think about all the other things everyone else in the world is going through and yes, we saw some shit, we went through some shit, and maybe we can help someone else because of it. I also embrace not being afraid to say that it wasn't perfect. It wasn't the worst, and it wasn't the best. We can help somebody else with our story.

Crystal: Because of your journey, you both have a solid foundation from which you will parent differently. The cycle has been broken.

Tyler: Having parents in your life that were more highly reactive than most people, normal people, I would say forces you to be more in tune with people's emotions. You pick up on some markers that other people might not. It is a *feel* thing too, some sort of like emotional sixth sense.

Crystal: Yes, it is a hypervigilance, and extreme state of being aware. I like the example of accidentally touching the hot stove and it burns us because it is hot. We will most likely figure out how to avoid touching the hot stove after it burns us, because it *freaking* hurts!

Moving on to the next question, what do you wish was different about your childhood?

Alex: I still say nothing. I am thankful for the things that shaped me into who I am. I can always say how I wish that we had more money, or we did this, and we did that, but ultimately, I don't. I would not be the person I am. I would not have the story to share. I would not have the compassion I do. I would not change the way that we were brought up at all.

Tyler: I agree. Alex hit it on the head when she said we wouldn't be the people we are today; we are the total sum of our experiences. To take away or change any of those experiences would make us not ourselves anymore. I would not change anything if I had the opportunity now.

Crystal: What you both said, from a life coach perspective is the key to not being stuck in victim mindset. It is key. I spent a lot of years in this victim mindset until I finally realized, okay, all that happened and look at ME! If that did not happen, I wouldn't be me and I am a passionate woman, making her dreams come true.

Alex: Our conversation yesterday blew my mind. I experienced a lot of growth in that conversation. I had a lot of emotion that hit me out of nowhere. Being able to talk to Tyler about some of our childhood things allowed me to be able to move through those memories. I had a *poor me sufferer* mindset when it came to that subject. I have been feeling sorry for myself and guilt for the feelings that I have had for years. Between yesterday's conversation and today's conversation, I am not sure what happened, but I have had a great night of sleep. It was huge to just be able to go to sleep and not have to worry about this fear of what Tyler felt or didn't feel about the situation, or what did Tyler know or didn't know about the situation.

Crystal: What I am hearing is you've been carrying this freaking burden for a long time and I didn't even know that this was weighing on you. You did so good by releasing that.

Alex: I also realized I am fear driven. I thought about that today a lot. The decisions that I make are from fear in many aspects of my life from personal to work. I am driven by fear. I choose not to do something because I am fearful of the outcome. I feel like that is because I've seen a lot of outcomes and they haven't all been positive, and I'm fearful that the choices that I make may negatively impact me.

Crystal: I acknowledge that because I spent a lot of time in addiction during your childhood, breaking promises, doing what I said I would not do, that caused fear. I see now that it was hard for you to believe that Chief Dreamweaver was real. I can imagine you saying, "Is she going to really be this person?" Maybe yesterday's conversation is the shift for you to live your life without fear. Release yourself from thinking that your life is going to look like mine did because it's not. Your life is nothing like mine was. Nothing about how you live your life is like mine.

Tyler: Alex saying that she was fear driven helped me connect the dots together in my life. I see a lot of the same behavior in myself. I fear making any kind of commitment.

Crystal: Now all three of us get to rewrite the story and encourage and build each other up so that we walk through fear.

This is the final question, and then you two can say whatever you want. What advice would you give to other young people growing up?

Tyler: Learn how to be comfortable with your own company because with current events, we are going to be spending a lot of time by ourselves at home. And with the way the world is heading, people spend less time together in person. If you're not comfortable with your own company, you're going to be searching for something to fill the gap all the time, and that's not healthy.

Alex: Be transparent. Mom, you were brutally honest with us with a lot of things and showed us a lot of things and you did not sugarcoat it or hide it from us. I think that no matter how hard that is, it leads to an open conversation and dialogue in relationships. I agree with and acknowledge what Tyler said regarding being comfortable with your own company.

Being honest with my feelings, especially with Tyler, is something I want to try to do more of. It is empowering to know that someone else has experienced what you're experiencing. Sometimes I am embarrassed of the struggles or the things I've had to do in my life. Embarrassed of going to the doctor because I didn't sleep for five days, not being able to drive my car because of anxiety and panic. All those things I think, darn my brother's probably experiencing these same things and we can help each other out. But instead fear and pride got in my way of being able to connect on that level.

Crystal: We have all talked about how we don't need anyone, how it's good to be okay with yourself and best to find love within, and THEN how it felt good to need each other. It is this weird dichotomy between needing people and being worthy of support. It is important to talk about mental health. I have struggled with mental health issues my whole life. In the book, I talk about this relationship with suicide that I thought everybody had. It was not until much later in life I learned that not everybody feels so distraught that they have always got an exit plan. So, we get to talk about that because we are in the middle of an epidemic of mental health crises. Just like what Alex said, it helps to know people understand where you are coming from and that you're not crazy, and you are not alone, you're someone experiencing dis-ease.

Well, we have answered all the questions. I feel like there is an ending looming. What is your final thought? Bring this home Kids! What is the weave!

Alex: Relief. I feel relief having finished the Zoom. I feel relief at being able to express ourselves. We expressed more things in the last two nights than maybe in my whole life. A huge relief and a lot of doors opened for different relationships.

Tyler: Relief. A good word for it. I feel closer to you guys for sure.

Alex: Agreed, which is weird because I was not sure that I'd ever get back to that point of feeling like I could relate to Ty. I had to put a wall up because I had beat myself up so much from walking out of the situation, and now it's like the door has opened back up and I have a long-lost sibling, which is a little weird to say.

Crystal: I think I will end with that. There is one face missing on this screen that is a part of the four of us who experienced some of the same trauma. We get to figure out how to support him as well.

Alex: Yes, I agree, and I think that this Zoom call would not be appropriate for him at 13-years-old anyway. So, it is not an exclusion, it's knowing that he's going to read the book and he is going to learn things in due time. He is always a part of the family.

Tyler: Agree, and to give my perspective for all this, I was that age not too long ago and Alex knocked it out of the park. I don't think this call would have been appropriate for him.

Crystal: I love you both from the bottom of my heart and will cherish this conversation forever.

Wow, here is the end. When you as a parent can sit here and be coached by your kids because they're so freaking smart and wise, you have arrived!

WRAP UP. WHAT IS NEXT?

Well reader, we did it. I spoke my truth and so did the important people in my life. Where do you need to speak your truth? What holds you back from dreaming, declaring, and delivering on your best life? I am not magical; this process is available to everyone. The key for me was support in my journey. I was not always aware of that, and in hindsight it is clear that it was crucial. The changes are definitely ours to make and the work ours to do, and with the loving support of mentors and coaches along the way, I was able to find my way, and so can you!

If you are inspired to up-level, leap into a heightened level of your life, reach out to me! You are worthy of all the things in life you dream of having. I would love to get to know you and your story with the intent of walking beside you as you rewrite any part that is holding you back. My best advice to you is to close this book, go to your computer, jump on my website www.dreamweaver. consulting and send me an email today.

I am on a mission to empower Dreamweavers, so let's set up your free consult to explore all your possibilities. Dreamweaver is where dreams are called forth, lived out, and brought into existence. Dreamweaver is about creating happy lives where dreams are discovered and embraced. I believe it all begins with true leadership. Leadership that elicits cooperation with others, where people want to come on board. Dreamweaver believes that only with a victim-free mindset and feeling worthy can we create the life of our dreams.

Dreamweaver is for:

- dreamers who want to start a new career or add a side hustle
- dreamers dreaming of new businesses or starting a dreamy nonprofit
- dreamers who have projects that need to be completed
- dreamers who have fitness goals to reach
- dreamers who have relationships to strengthen
- college students preparing to graduate and dreaming of their careers
- high school students dreaming of their next steps after graduation
- dreamers who want to determine "their" dream
- businesses dreaming of increasing employee morale, retention, and productivity
- teams dreaming of creating amazing camaraderie and bonding
- families working on deeper connection through understanding and supporting each other's dreams
- post-secondary education entities looking to support students in making all their dreams come true

- sober support groups looking to bring dreaming, declaring, and delivering goals into recovery
- You!

To best support you in your journey, let me share how I see my role as Chief Dreamweaver in your full life transformation process:

- I see myself walking beside you in your process of moving forward.
- I see my coaching relationship with you beginning after you 100% choose into it.
- I see myself supporting you from a place of being unattached to your reactions, or the result you achieve.
- I see myself lovingly shining a light on areas you are unable to see.
- I see myself listening to the language and nonverbal cues you give me, to guide the direction of my feedback.
- I see myself guiding you to see the blocks holding you back.
- I see myself maintaining healthy boundaries to allow you to experience your own breakthroughs.
- I see myself celebrating the transformation wins created by you.
- Reach out today and let us begin launching your dreams.

EPILOGUE

Right now, as I write this book, following a successful Bestseller in a Weekend® training with Alicia Dunams, the world is at the very beginning of a pandemic that will be forever marked in history. I am sure everybody will be weaving the isolation and uncertainty of the pandemic into their life stories from this point forward. During the pandemic the entire world, region by region, began "sheltering in place" and "quarantining" in various degrees. It was a stressful time for many and a gift to the world as well.

We as humans were given the opportunity to look at how we spend time and what and who we value. Following the guidelines of shelter-in-place means to stay in your home, venture out only for essential items and when you do, stay six feet apart from other humans. Businesses deemed as non-essential have been directed to close, restaurants and stores that are labeled essential, have begun following new safety precautions to include masking to keep from spreading the deadly virus.

I have observed many struggles for the workers and businesses deemed nonessential. First, is the loss of income and the fear around losing something you have spent your hard-earned time and money to build.

The second, is a loss of feeling valued in the world, as defined by the word "nonessential."

The reason I will also mention the gifts is that this pandemic has forced humans to slow down, spend quiet time, and minimize travel, greatly reducing the carbon footprint. The effects are profound for humans and our earth. Some people are struggling, some people are finding peace. The earth is recovering and glowing with cleaner air, bluer skies, fresher smells, and an influx of animal movement.

As a transformation life coach and consultant, it has given me the opportunity to stop, back off from the crazy pace of my life, and support myself and others as we make a global shift in how we live.

One of my biggest blessings has been the space and quiet time to let my brain rest and my story unfold. I have been designing it in my head for several years now, which is the perfect segue into the epilogue. Bestseller in a Weekend® was an incredible experience gifted to me during the pandemic, as I mentioned earlier in this book. I am grateful I was encouraged to tell my story. Thank you, Alicia Dunams.

And, for all you readers out there curious about more of the stories touched on this book, I have great news! There will be at least three more books to come based on the Evolution of Dreamweaver. Once my daughter Alex, and son Tyler do the

Dreamweaver process with me (yes, I am declaring this will happen!) that will unfold into two more books detailing their experiences of breaking unhealthy generational cycles. The fourth book in the Evolution of Dreamweaver will be the youngest child's experience when he reads and processes the first three books. And yes, I am declaring that will happen as well. I must give credit where credit is due to my final peer reader, who I chose upon the recommendation of my book writing coach Alicia Dunams. She suggested I choose someone I trusted, who had not read the book yet, to read it the final time before I submit for type setting and proof reading. Jennifer was my girl! She is a friend that goes back to the Jr. High (we called it that back then) days of "natural helper" camp, playing competitively against each other in high school softball, working together during my crazy 21 year old phase, knowing my first love, and coming back full circle to do the Dreamweaver process with me. She was absolutely the perfect person to read the advance copy proof. She gave me feedback and ideas, that I "thought" I was open to hearing and had some resistance too because I was feeling sensitive about my writing. We talked on the phone and here is what Jennifer shared with me, she reminded me that this book is a necessary story to be shared with the world. She raved about the flow, and said that the strategy of weaving Grandma, Jake and Crystal into each chapter was phenomenal. She did however miss Grandma in Chapters three and four, so you can thank Jennifer for those gems of additions! She also suggested breaking Chapter 8 up into two chapters because the first part of the chapter felt so "victorious" for her to read! Jennifer felt all my pain release, leaving me revived, and alive. She referenced "girl on fire" and painted the visual of me stretching out of my old skin and regrowing. Again, good call, the chapter titled victorious now lives!

A few other interesting thoughts Jennifer shared with me are how much she could identify with each character in the story from Jake, to Grandma, to Jake's Mom and Jake's husband and that she admired how I chose not to blame in the story, and embrace that it happened for me. In the larger sense, the book allowed her to see that her life has also happened for her, a particularly important shift out of victim-mindset.

I loved how she shared how she felt Grandma sets the foundation of the story with her love of carpet, a very symbolic thought as carpet eventually covers the foundation of a home and the time Grandma and I sat in the carpeted garage most likely created my love of "sitting spaces." Sitting spaces are places I sit and receive downloads of information that I often share in live videos. As our feedback conversation ended, Jennifer and I talked about the Tyler and Alex chapter and how she was missing Cooper. My third, and youngest child. She made a profound suggestion, that I am going to do. She suggested talking with Cooper (I will do a recorded Zoom with him) and capturing what his thoughts are about me writing the book. She is aware he doesn't know my story, and she also pointed out that he may know more than I think, and it would be really cool to get his thoughts recorded from the 13 year old perspective so that when he does read the book, I will have the comparison from thirteen to whatever age he reads it. It will also serve as a perfect introduction to Cooper's Evolution of Dreamweaver book.

This is the point in Jennifer and my conversation where I break down and cry because she points out that she could hear Alex and Tyler in their chapter, and actually visualize them, she saw Alex with an iced latte and Tyler as the laid back mellow "man of many words" that he is. She talked about what amazing humans they are. She acknowledged me for my incredible job parenting and that it was even reflected in the non-hostile situation where Cooper went to live with his Dad. She pointed out that Cooper was able to follow his heart from the lessons he was taught by me, and that he was able to speak his needs and choose to live with his Dad. Through tear filled eyes, I thanked Jennifer for her loving feedback and shared that hearing my kids acknowledge me was life-changing, and that if nothing more ever came from this book, that was enough!

Lastly, I am currently in the process of creating a coffee table version of my poetry that I spoke of in previous chapters. It is dark poetry that was a necessary means of expressing myself during the early years. I chose not to include any of it in this book, as I want you, the reader to walk away feeling as victorious as I do in this moment. This coffee table book will include pictures of the original poems, written in my hand, most likely accompanied by a typed version. Stay tuned!

One final word of gratitude and love.

I am grateful for me, Crystal Dawn Church. I am grateful that I have lived the life I have lived and that I have been gifted the ability to heal others with my Dreamweaver talents. I am grateful for those that I have met along the way that have shaped who I am, and for all those yet to come. I am a loving, joyous, powerful woman who is worthy of living the life of my dreams.

AUTHOR'S BIO

The Evolution of DREAMWEAVER: 7 Steps to Delivering on Your Dreams is for anyone who is ready to create a powerful life, step into a victim-free mindset, embrace self-worth, understand you have the power to create your dreams, and live for yourself.

As a graduate of Central Washington University, with a Bachelor of Science degree in community health education, and more importantly, a masters in the school of hard knocks, I have selected for myself the title of Chief Dreamweaver. I have given myself unlimited power to create, make my dreams a reality, and live for myself. Even during the challenging times in my life, I have always been dreaming, declaring, and delivering.

I am a mother, a single parent of three. I am a person in long term recovery from addictions, 14 years in 2020. I was the Executive Director of a nationally recognized youth mentor program for seven years, a nonprofit that I brought back to life. I am the 2020 chair of the Kittitas County Law and Justice Council, a Rotary Club member and Changemaker award winner. I am one of the founders of the first local nonprofit network in my community of Ellensburg, Washington, and I am the founder and CEO of Dreamweaver Consulting. I am the author of my story, *The Evolution of Dreamweaver: 7 Steps to Delivering on Your Dreams.*

Made in the USA
Monee, IL
29 March 2021

64253913R00095